T0043355

SAN
TOR
INI

**Travel with Marco Polo
Insider Tips**

INSIDER TIP
**Your shortcut
to a great
experience**

MARCO POLO
TOP HIGHLIGHTS

PREHISTORIC MUSEUM ⭐

Small but highly informative; here you can learn everything you want to know about Santorini 3,500 years ago

📷 *Tip: Only photos without flash or stand/tripod are allowed.*

➤ p. 43, Firá & Around

VOLKAN ON THE ROCKS ⭐2

You will hardly find a more beautiful view of the island's capital Firá than from this restaurant – and food and drinks are first class.

➤ p. 52, Firá & Around

ANCIENT THERA ⭐3

The ruins of this antique city are located on a long cape high above the sea.

📷 *Tip: The scenery is particularly exciting, with aeroplanes landing in the background.*

➤ p. 69, Kamári & the Centre

PANAGÍA EPISKOPÍ ⭐4

Even those who don't like churches will be enchanted by the many flowers in the courtyard of the oldest church on the island, and by its absolute tranquillity.

📷 *Tip: Talk to the couple who are the church wardens and they will be happy to have their picture taken with you.*

➤ p. 71, Kamári & the Centre

PÝRGOS ⭐5

Winding lanes with hardly a shop in sight lead uphill to the castle, from where there are fabulous views of the entire island that you may be able to enjoy by yourself – even at sunset.

➤ p. 75, Kamári & the Centre

FÁROS (LIGHTHOUSE) ⭐ 8

From the lighthouse, your gaze leads you across the sea into the entire caldera and towards Crete. The wild feel of this place is reminiscent of the coastlines of Ireland or Norway.

➤ p. 95, Políssa & the South

EXCAVATIONS IN AKROTÍRI 6

Some think that this, the oldest city in Europe, was the legendary Atlantis. It feels as if Minoans could come round the corner at any moment.

➤ p. 93, Políssa & the South

LÓNDSA FORT ⭐ 9

Stroll through beautiful Oía up to this castle ruin, which is now a popular viewpoint.

➤ p. 100, Oía & the North

RED BEACH (PARALÍA KÓKKINI) ⭐ 7

Red lava gravel and red cliffs: this beach is truly unique. You can get there either on foot or by boat.
📷 *Tip: Walking there is a great experience. The best photos are taken from the spot where the beach first comes into sight.*

➤ p. 93, Políssa & the South

AMMOÚDI 10

Flanked by bizarre lava cliffs and the sea, the narrow pier is full of the fish tavernas' tables, set in front of a backdrop of small boats (see photo).
📷 *Tip: The most authentic images can be taken in the evening when the popular tavernas are packed with people.*

➤ p. 100, Oía & the North

CONTENTS

OÍA & THE NORTH

FIRÁ & AROUND

KAMÁRI & THE CENTRE

PERÍSSA & THE SOUTH

CONTENTS

⏱	Plan your visit	🍴 Eating/drinking	🛕 Rainy day activities
€–€€€	Price categories	🛍 Shopping	🐷 Budget activities
(*)	Premium-rate phone number	🍸 Going out	👪 Family activities
		🏖 Top beaches	🚩 Classic experiences

(🕮 A2) Refers to the removable pull-out map
(0) Located off the map

BEST OF
SANTORINI

Heavenly churches: from Oía you have a view of the caldera

BEST ☂

WHEN IT RAINS

ACTIVITIES TO BRIGHTEN YOUR DAY

TAKE A DIVE

Outsmart the rain and head under water: the *Santorini Dive Center* in Maríssa offers diving trips to the sea-drowned caldera

➤ p. 34, Sport & Activities

ANOTHER WORLD

Visitors to the *Orthodox Cathedral* in Firá will be transported from this world with its bad weather days into another. If you take your time to study the cathedral's vast wall paintings, you'll immerse yourself in the island's rich religious tradition (photo).

➤ p. 44, Firá & Around

BECOME A WINE CONNOISSEUR

The history and culture of wine-growing on Santorini is exhibited in the pumice-stone galleries of the wine museum at *Lava-Koutsoyianópoulos Winery* between Kamári and Messariá. Visitors can also taste the wines.

➤ p. 73, Kamári & the Centre

SHOPPING IN MÉGALOCHÓRI

You won't find tourist coaches parked in front of the five ceramic workshops and artist studios in *Mégalochóri*. Although some of the exhibitions resemble those you might find in a museum, admission is free. The artists are happy to talk to you, and everything is in close proximity.

➤ p. 79, Kamári & the Centre

NATURAL SPECTACLE AT THE HEADLAND

It's worth visiting the *lighthouse* on the promontory at Akrotíri in the island's southwest even in wind and rain. Experience the force of nature with windswept trees, strong gusts of wind, spray from the sea's waves and low-lying clouds. This place becomes truly exciting when Zeus, King of the Gods, is casting thunderbolts across the horizon!

➤ p. 95, Maríssa & the South

BEST 🐷
ON A BUDGET

FOOD FROM THE BAKER

Most villages on the island have a bakery, some of which are open round the clock. Here, bakeries sell a wide range of food, beyond bread and cakes. Try the delicious strudel-dough pastries called *píttes*; they come filled with spinach and/or cheese, a hot dog-type sausage or semolina. And enjoy the wonderful views with a cup of coffee.

FERRY TO THIRASÍA

Early morning on almost every day of the week, a small boat ferries adventurous tourists and workers from Oía to Ríva on the neighbouring island of *Thirasía* (see photo). This free service returns to Oía in the afternoon. The captain will give you the exact times.
➤ p. 106, Oía & the North

GYROS AL FRESCO

In Firá you can get gyros in the *platía*, in Oía at the bus terminal and in Kamári at the beach promenade, where they also sell small meat skewers called *kalamákia*. Four are more than enough, as there are always fries on the side.

FREE FOLKLORE

There is a parish festival in some village on Santorini almost every week. Here you can experience authentic island living for free – often accompanied by processions, dancing and music. The small churches are beautifully decorated with flags and banners, and visitors – whether they are churchgoers or not – are served food and drink free of charge.

LOW-COST CALDERA VIEW

Usually, a meal with caldera views comes at a price on Santorini, but there are still exceptions: the excellent *Náoussa* taverna in Firá and the more average *Nocturna* in Oía offer beautiful views at reasonable prices.
➤ p. 51, Firá & Around, p. 103, Oía & the North

BEST

WITH CHILDREN

DRINKS FOR KIDS

Are your little ones jealous of the colourful cocktails that you love to drink? Then non-alcoholic mocktails are just the thing and are available in most bars and cafés.

CABLE-CAR RIDE

A *ride in the cable car* from Firá to the old port of Skála is a bit of an adventure if you enter the first or last of the interlinked cabins. You can always make part of the journey with a mule, if there is not too much of a queue.
➤ p. 47, Firá & Around

SAND-CASTLE PIONEERS

Building sand castles is unusual on Santorini, but maybe your children would like to volunteer? The sand on *Políssa Beach* is better suited for this activity than anywhere else on the island. Perhaps some of the Greek children will find this fun, too!
➤ p. 86, Políssa & the South

BEACH VOLLEYBALL

Older children may also like to play beach volleyball, and there are courts not only on the sandy beach at Políssa but also by *Théros Wave Bar,* south of Vlicháda. People to play with are easy to find, and the courts can be used free of charge. Parents can order a cold drink while watching the sporting prowess of their youngsters below.
➤ p. 89, Políssa & the South

FOR COWBOYS AND GIRLS

Guided hacks in the rough lava landscape of Akrotíri will make little riders feel as if they are in the Wild West. On top of that, a short beach ride is included in the programme. *Santo Horse-Riding* are the children's riding experts, and no previous experience is required. Please book in advance.
➤ p. 91, Políssa & the South

BEST

CLASSIC EXPERIENCES

ONLY ON SANTORINI

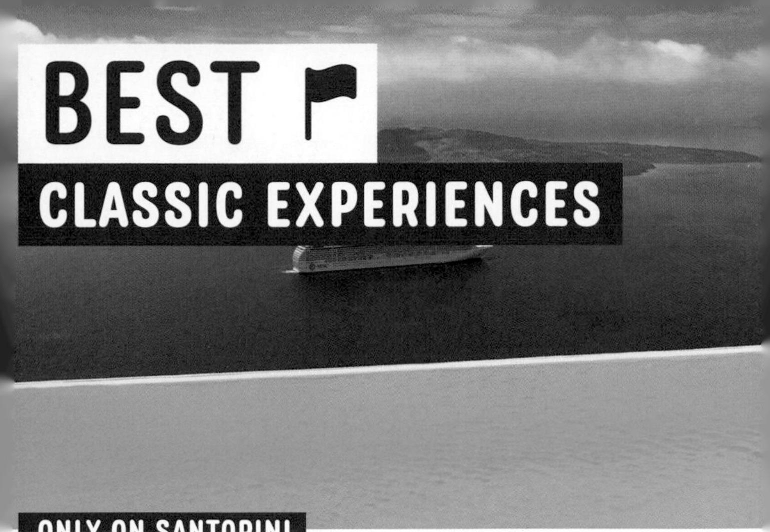

INFINITY POOLS

All superior accommodation on the caldera edge has its own infinity pool, where sky and water seem to blend into each other. The experience of swimming in them and seemingly becoming one with the Aegean is wonderful (see photo).

EATING WITHOUT A VIEW

Local people see the caldera every day anyway, which is why they like to visit restaurants on main roads that are avoided by most tourists. The food here is authentic and very reasonably priced. An example is *Kyrá Níki* outside Firá.

➤ p. 50, Firá & Around

HOME OF THE DEAD

Santorini's graveyards, such as the one in Vourvoúlos, resemble small villages consisting exclusively of chapels. The ossuaries, which are mostly unlocked, serve as the final resting place of generations of human skeletal remains. Please act respectfully when visiting.

➤ p. 57, Firá & Around

FOCUS ON TOMATOES

There is no industry on Santorini these days, but the tall chimneys of former tomato-paste factories remain. The *factory in Vlicháda* is now an industrial museum and art gallery: here you can learn interesting facts about Santorini's social history.

➤ p. 88, Períssa & the South

FISHERMEN'S CAVES

The fishermen of Santorini once carved out caves from the soft rock to store their boats and fishing equipment. In Akrotíri, many of these niches have been transformed into tavernas; the *Melina's Tavern* even has its own art gallery.

➤ p. 91, Períssa & the South

GET TO KNOW SANTORINI

Whatever the choice of vessel, everyone wants to spend time on the water

DISCOVER SANTORINI

On arrival: the white houses of Firá can be seen from a great distance

Ships do not simply dock along the coast of Santorini; they sail straight into the centre of the island. If approaching from the north, your ferry will edge through a 2-km / 1.2-mile strait which separates the main island of Santorini from its smaller neighbour Thirasía. You'll see the island's steep cliffs soaring up 360m / 1,180ft in front of you, in all shades of white, grey, red and brown – you have just sailed into an enormous volcanic crater.

AMAZING VILLAGES

High above the sea, a kilometre-long strip of whitewashed houses clings to the clifftop. These are the larger caldera-edge villages of Oía and Firá, with the neighbouring settlements of Firostefáni and Imerovígli. The inhabitants of Oía and Firá not only built on the steep slope of the caldera, but also carved out the walls of

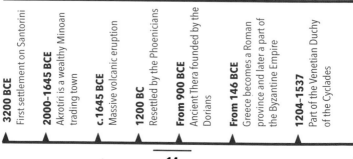

3200 BCE
First settlement on Santorini

2000–1645 BCE
Akrotíri is a wealthy Minoan trading town

c.1645 BCE
Massive volcanic eruption

1200 BC
Resettled by the Phoenicians

From 900 BCE
Ancient Thera founded by the Dorians

From 146 BCE
Greece becomes a Roman province and later a part of the Byzantine Empire

1204–1537
Part of the Venetian Duchy of the Cyclades

the crater to create cave dwellings and, with growing tourism, hotels and small swimming pools.

Your ferry sails past Oía towards Néa and Paléa Kaméni, two bare, lava outcrops in the centre of the caldera. It will anchor at one of the most unique ports in the world; its narrow dock nestles below a 300-m / 984-ft high cliff which vehicles drive up via a precariously steep road with lots of hairpin bends. On reaching the top of the crater, Santorini reveals its other, less rugged side: gentle, vine-covered hills spill gradually down to resorts along the east coastline and the open sea.

WE WILL BE LANDING IN A MINUTE

Santorini's airport is situated near the coast on the less dramatic part of the island. Those approaching by plane will be treated to Santorini's unique beauty from a bird's eye perspective. As most flights arrive from the south, one of Santorini's landmarks is visible on the left shortly before landing: the 567-m / 1,860-ft high Profítis Ilías mountain rising up from the coastal plain. This non-volcanic limestone and marble formation is far older than the rest of the island.

BIRTH OF AN ISLAND

Profítis Ilías dates back many millions of years and, until approximately 1.5 million years ago, stood alone in the middle of the Aegean. Volcanic activity then occurred in the seabed, followed by a series of eruptions over millenia to create an almost circular volcanic island. In its centre towered a volcanic cone up to

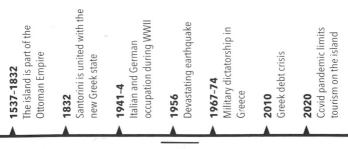

1537–1832
The island is part of the Ottoman Empire

1832
Santorini is united with the new Greek state

1941-4
Italian and German occupation during WWII

1956
Devastating earthquake

1967-74
Military dictatorship in Greece

2010
Greek debt crisis

2020
Covid pandemic limits tourism on the island

1,700m / 5,577ft in height; this was later destroyed by a massive eruption within the cone itself, causing the collapse of the island between the headland of Akrotíri, the present site of the lighthouse, and Aspronísi. This collapse left a huge volcanic crater, the caldera, and formed a new channel for the sea to enter. Another devastating volcanic eruption around 1600 BCE destroyed another section of the ring between Oía and Thirasía to form Santorini's present shape. The eruption left layers of pumice and ash deposits up to 60m / 200ft deep, which still cover the island today, and may have caused the first European city to be buried under lava and ash. Since 1967, archaeologists have been excavating well-preserved remains near the village of Akrotíri in the southwest of Santorini.

A SMALL ISLAND, BUT A HUGE TOURIST DESTINATION

Despite a total area of only 74.4km² / 28.7 sq miles, Santorini is diverse with much to offer. From Oía in the north to the lighthouse on the headland of Akrotíri, you can drive for 27km / 16 miles along the caldera edge. The capital Firá lies just 10–15km / 6–9 miles from the island's main resorts, Kamári and Eríssa. Although Santorini has a population of just 15,550, its hotels, B&Bs and apartment complexes together offer almost the same number of beds. The island also welcomes thousands of cruise-ship passengers every year. The luxury liners dock at barrels located off the coast of Firá because the caldera is too deep for them to anchor.

A DIFFERENT BEACH EXPERIENCE

Almost all of Santorini's beaches are situated along the stretches of coast bordering the open sea to the east and southeast. The three main beaches are a mix of black and grey coarse lava sand with pebbles, and cover several kilometres. Baxédes Beach in the north is virtually unspoilt, while the promenades along the beach between Monólithos and Kamári and between Eríssa and Vlicháda are populated with hotels, B&Bs and tavernas. You can, however, still find sections of beach without any parasol or lounger hire. The south coast offers more secluded beaches, accessed along dirt tracks which often lead down to a solitary beachside taverna. These beaches are mainly covered in coarse volcanic rocks, pebbles and pumice, making it difficult for bathers to enter the sea. Their appeal lies in their beautiful natural backdrop: steep cliffs of multi-coloured volcanic ash.

INSIDER TIP
The quiet Santorini

UNUSUAL WINES

There is very little agriculture left on the island, with land being turned over more and more to wineries and vineyards. Santorini's wines are outstanding and prized for their flavour. The grapes are grown on low-spiralling vines close to the lava soil which collects moisture from the dew and reflects the sunlight. You can taste the results of these favourable conditions at one of the island's many wineries – another way of discovering Santorini's uniqueness.

AT A GLANCE

15,500
population

Isle of Wight: 142,000

>900,000

cruise ship passengers visit Firá each year

**69km /
43 miles**
coastline

Isle of Wight: 92km / 57 miles

**74.4km² /
28.7 sq miles**
area

Isle of Wight: 384km² / 148 sq miles

**HIGHEST PEAK:
PROFÍTIS ILÍAS**

**567m /
1,860ft**

Scafell Pike
978m / 3,209ft

**MOST POPULAR
MONTHS FOR
VISITORS:**

**JULY/
AUGUST**

**THE
CALDERA
IS UP TO**

**400m /
1,300ft**

DEEP

ΣΑΝΤΟΡΙΝΗ

This is how Santorini is spelled in Greek

THIRÁ

is the original Greek name for the island, with the A being stressed

**NIKTÉRI, BROÙSKO &
VISÁNTO**
are the island's wine varieties

**120
ISLAND EMPLOYEES ARE
RESPONSIBLE FOR CLEARING
RUBBISH ON SANTORINI**

UNDERSTAND SANTORINI

AGÍA, ÁGII, ÁGIOS

You will come across these three little words often on your travels in Greece. They form part of the names of villages, churches and monasteries, as well as of fishing boats and ferries. *Agía* is a female saint, *Ágios* a male saint and *Ágii* the plural form. The Blessed Virgin Mary is honoured with a special title; she is referred to as the *Panagía*, the "All-Holy".

ARCHITECTURE

The people of Santorini live on and also inside the ground. Before the earthquake struck in 1956, cave apartments were the most popular type of housing on the island. The soft pumice in the crater rock and on the gorge ridges made it easy for the locals to carve out niches and build dry, sheltered and affordable dwellings protected from earthquakes. The air-filled pumice is also prized because of its high insulation, providing coolness in summer and warmth in winter.

However, more affluent inhabitants have constructed solid houses made of imported wood and stone since medieval times. Originally built around hilltops without any windows in their walls, these houses lined up in a row to form a kind of wall around the village. Good examples can still be seen in Emborió and Pýrgos. After the island had fought off the threat of pirates in the 18th century and was allowed to unite with the newly founded Greek State in 1834, more and more people began settling on the ridge overlooking the caldera. Neoclassical, multi-storey buildings were built above the old cave dwellings, which you can still see today, particularly in Oía.

Many of these villas and houses were destroyed by the earthquake in 1956, and reconstruction involved tonnes of concrete and little imagination. Once whitewashed and limewashed however, these clusters of traditionally flat-roofed Cycladic houses – with the occasional barrel vault roof in between – create villages that blend perfectly with the landscape around.

ATLANTIS – FACT OR FICTION?

Ever since the fifth century BCE when the Greek philosopher Plato mentioned the legend of Atantis in his dialogic works *Timaeus* and *Critias*, people have speculated on the location of this once prosperous island that was allegedly submerged in the distant past. A theory, favoured by many, drew comparisons between Plato's Atlantis and Santorini, since the island had been devastated by a volcanic eruption long ago. There is just one problem with this theory: according to Plato's description, Atlantis was located "beyond the Pillars of Hercules" – the Strait of Gibraltar. Nobody is sure where Plato got his information; had he simply been listening to ancient legends or was the island and its downfall simply a product of his imagination?

ECONOMIC CRISIS

The deep economic and financial crisis that has gripped Greece since 2011 has left little trace on Santorini. Of course, the pensions and salaries of civil servants have been cut on the island, as on the mainland, and VAT rates have risen considerably. The drastic increase in petrol prices and the rising cost of living do not go unnoticed – yet still, Santorini's economy continues to flourish – by relying solely on high-end tourism. Santorini has always attracted the type of Greek and international tourist who is least affected by drastic austerity measures and tax changes. As everywhere in Greece, restaurant and bar owners have exercised a great deal of restraint in setting their prices – even if they are far higher here than elsewhere.

FLAGS

A second flag is often hoisted in front of churches alongside the white-and-blue Greek national flag. This is the official flag of the Greek Orthodox Church and shows a black Byzantine double-headed eagle on a yellow background. Its strong resemblance to the former flag of the Byzantine Empire, which Santorini was part of until 1204 and which was destroyed by the Ottomans in 1453, means it is not seen in front of government and administrative buildings. There you will see the flag of the European Union, with its characteristic 12 golden stars flying in the wind. A sure sign that Greece is looking to the future!

The island's wineries await!

GORGES

While all tourists are captivated by the caldera, there is a second characteristic element of Santorini's landscape which is noticed only by few people: the numerous gorges.

The geology in Santorini's east is characterised by gorges cut into the steep pumice cliffs which run from just below the caldera ridge out to sea. They have been eroded by water over the last 3,500 years. The frequent torrential rainfall in winter is drained along channels that cut through the surface and gradually wear away the rock. The island's inhabitants have used this knowledge over the

Santorini's colours are those of sky and sea – white and blue

just enjoying a walk. They are allowed to marry as celibacy is only required from the rank of bishop upwards. There are three other things which every *pappás* needs: a stiff hat, long hair and a proper beard. Hair loss appears to be rare – probably a sign of a healthy lifestyle. *Pappádes* can be seen frequently, even in bars, cafés and tavernas. Their job is secure even in a crisis, because they are employed by the Greek state.

There is no church tax in Hellas and no issue with people leaving the Church. Almost 98 per cent of Greeks belong to the Greek Orthodox Church. They developed their fundamental beliefs on the basis of early Christianity, and have left them unchanged since the 9th century. In Greece, the Pope is not regarded as the head of Christendom.

OVERTOURISM

Overtourism is the superlative of mass tourism. Venice has become a victim of its own success as a tourist destination, and Santorini isn't far behind, recording more than six million overnight stays annually. Therefore, the island is attempting to limit the number of cruise-ship passengers to 12,000 per day. On the other hand, winter tourism is promoted, the airport has recently been expanded and there are no restrictions on building new hotels.

Tourism has resulted in an increase in the cost of living for local people. Airbnb and similar developments are making existing housing problems worse. Housing for poorer families

centuries to build cave dwellings and houses in the pumice cliffs as hideaways from pirates roaming at sea; the fertile soil above the ground could then be put to good use. Vóthonas is one of the nicest examples of a gorge settlement.

LONG HAIR AND A BEARD

Orthodox priests always wear their dark gowns, even if they are out shopping with their wife and children or and the many workers from abroad who service the hotel and catering industries is becoming increasingly short in supply because holidaymakers pay more for a room per night than a normal person's weekly rent.

The crowds of tourists are also causing environmental issues. While the household rubbish can be stored for a few more years in former mines, hazardous waste has to be shipped to Piraeus. Drinking water is sourced from wells which are up to 80m / 260ft deep, leading to an ever-dropping ground water table. Two sea-water desalination plants are high energy consumers. Clear sea water along the coast is ensured by five communal waste water treatment plants, all of which direct the treated waste water into the Aegean through long pipelines.

POZZUOLANA

The brightly coloured layers of pumice covering Santorini were for centuries the island's most profitable asset. Enormous quantities of pumice were excavated, transported down chutes built into the caldera and loaded directly onto cargo ships waiting in the harbour. It was then processed into pozzolana, also known as Santorini earth. When mixed eight-to-one with lime and a little water, this pumice powder forms a cement that hardens with water and is resistant even to salt water. Because of these properties, it was used to build ports throughout the Eastern Mediterranean and also to construct the 163-km / 101-mile long Suez Canal between

TRUE OR FALSE?

SANTORINI IS EXPENSIVE

In August, two thirds of all hotel rooms cost more than 200 euros per night, but even then it is still possible to find accommodation for under 100 euros. Of course, such quarters won't come with a private infinity pool. As is the case everywhere, comfort and beauty come at a price. In particular, this applies to the hotels, restaurants and bars at the caldera edge. However, this sought-after strip of land has many low walls and park benches where you can have your picnic and open a bottle of wine while enjoying that fantastic view.

Exploring the island can be fun with an expensive hired open-top car, but equally enjoyable – and much cheaper – on the regular buses that serve the island.

ALL GREEKS LOVE DANCING THE SYRTÁKI

The movie classic *Zorbá the Greek,* with Anthony Quinn, made the *syrtáki* the most famous Greek dance around the world. In truth, the Greeks had never heard of it before! Today, it is a must-have during "Greek Nights" in beach hotels and tavernas, whereas at parish festivals you can watch real Greek dances, such as the *syrtós* and *hassápiko*. Otherwise, in the night clubs of Santorini, people dance to Greek rock music, as they would anywhere else.

1859 and 1869. The mining of pumice stopped on Santorini in 1990.

POWER ISSUES

Over 120,000 megawatts of electricity are consumed on Santorini every year. On a per-head-basis, this is five times more than in the UK. The high energy consumption is down to air conditioning systems and tourism. All this power is generated by a power station near Monólithos which burns the cheap Masut heating oil, a highly viscose residue from crude oil production that is harmful to the environment. Tankers deliver it to the island two to three times a month. At the current time, there are only two solar parks (in Messariá and Vourvoúlos). In addition, a few private properties are fitted with solar panels to feed electricity into the grid. There is no wind power at all because it is believed wind farms would spoil the scenery and deter tourists from coming to the island.

SAY YES

Santorini is becoming the dream wedding venue for an increasing number of couples. Wedding agencies can be hired locally to book priests or registrars, organise luxury limousines and photoshoots and order bouquets and champagne. The sky is the limit when it comes to choosing the location. Couples can stage their wedding on luxury yachts, in the active volcanic crater on Nea Kameni, on a beach or at a poolside, and even on the summit of Profítis Ilías. The most important thing is the subsequent photo shoot, which can last days.

WATCH YOUR LANGUAGE

Be careful not to use the "Nee" word on holiday on Santorini as it might have unintended con- sequences. Greeks say "Nee" when they get married: it means "yes". Also confusing is the frequently used word "Entáxi", which has nothing to do with taxis, but simply means "Okay".

INSIDER TIP
"Nee" means "yes"

WHITE AND BLUE

It is not absolutely clear why so many of the houses and chapels on Santorini and other Greek islands are painted in white and blue. Romanticists point out that white and blue are the primary colours of the sky and clouds, as well as of water and waves – natural elements that are omnipresent in Greece.

Analysts like to remind us of the blue and white present in the Greek national flag: painting their houses in these national colours in the 19th century was a way for the people of Santorini and other Cycladic islands to demonstrate their solidarity with the independent Greek State while other Aegean islands were still under Ottoman rule.

WINDS

Unlike Northern Europeans, the locals of Santorini don't have to look out of the window to find out what the weather is like. The forecast in summer is always sunny and warm. The wind is the only element of uncertainty, and can change constantly. The Greeks have a name for every type of breeze,

A cool home: traditional houses include cave apartments, like these in Vóthonas

depending on the season and direction from which it is blowing.

Summer welcomes the north wind, the *meltémi*, which blows gently in the early morning, gradually increasing in strength by lunchtime, to calm down by siesta time in late afternoon, only to reach its strongest in the evening. *Meltémi* winds can develop from a breeze into a storm without warning in a matter of minutes, throwing boats back to land and blowing pumice dust over the fields. This wind is not only feared by sailors; waiters also have to be on guard as it can throw sunshades, tables and chairs in the air.

For tourists, the *meltémi* can offer a respite from the stifling summer temperatures; it clears the air, allowing the island to bathe in the beautiful Aegean light again and bring the neighbouring islands seemingly close enough to touch.

WINERIES

Santorini wines are not only cultivated on volcanic soil, they are also left to ripen and mature in volcanic rock. The wineries are housed in kilometre-long caves and chambers carved out of the pumice stone where the temperature is kept constant. Some have entrances facing the crater, others face the gorges. Many of these wineries are open to the public and offer wine-tastings; some even provide information on their winegrowing history and culture.

EATING
SHOPPING
SPORT

The rugged cliffs of the caldera provide a striking backdrop

EATING & DRINKING

No other Greek island has as many gourmet restaurants as Santorini, many of which are located directly at the caldera's edge. In addition to their creative Mediterranean cuisine, they also have the most fabulous views.

Other eateries are to be found in the centre of local villages, and even in the lava caves of old wine cellars; and you will be able to find a great number of real Greek tavernas away from the expensive caldera-edge promenade. Santorini is now increasingly interested in catering to its many Chinese visitors, offering authentic Far Eastern cuisine as well as Mexican and Japanese food. Tourists on a budget will find the many gyros outlets and pizzerias to their satisfaction.

TOMATOES EVERYWHERE

Today there is little agriculture and livestock farming left on Santorini. Almost all cooking ingredients are sourced from other parts of Greece, and even the fish is predominantly imported, with prawns, crayfish and calamari often being flown in from other continents.

Despite this growing trend towards "globalisation", many chefs attempt to give a regional touch to their creations. They use the island's sun-dried small tomatoes, in particular, as well as the local fáva yellow peas, which are hardly known in the rest of Europe. Other typical ingredients comprise pickled capers complete with their stems and thorns!

TIME TO EAT

Santorini's international restaurants are much the same as those anywhere in the world; they have regular opening and closing hours, usually serving guests from 7pm or 8pm in the evening and sometimes for lunch

A great combination: a cold beer from the island (right) to go with tomato *keftedes* (left)

between 1pm and 4pm. In contrast, a traditional Greek taverna opens for breakfast at 9am and stays open until late in the evening serving warm food. In these places you will usually find a menu in several languages, but note only the dishes marked with a price are available. Any special dishes are either written in pencil on the menu in Greek or you have to ask the waiter.

Many restaurants on Santorini take table bookings and this is particularly recommended for places at the caldera edge and for all gourmet dining.

A LITTLE BIT OF EVERYTHING

Traditionally, Greeks do not usually order a set menu with several courses. Restaurants dedicated to tourists generally offer simple daytime menus, although that's not how Greek people eat. Most locals dislike going out to eat on their own or as a couple. Instead, they prefer the so-called *paréa*, which means a large group of friends and family gathering around the table. In a *paréa*, people don't order for themselves. One person will order several starters and salads for everyone sitting around the table who then serve themselves, selecting what they like and taking as much as they want. The same procedure is often followed for the main course, too, which is usually accompanied by a large sharing platter of fries.

Desserts virtually never appear on menus in basic Greek tavernas, yet there is a wide selection available in the more high-end restaurants. In a typical taverna, after a meal, the owner will serve fresh fruit on the house.

PAYING THE BILL

In Greece you don't give the waiter a tip by rounding up your bill; instead you should leave the tip discreetly on the table before getting up.

WINE ECONOMY

It is obvious to everyone at first glance that winegrowing dominates the Santorini landscape. Although it would be virtually impossible to taste all the island's wines on one holiday, it's worth trying by visiting some of the island's wineries that offer wine-tasting sessions (usually for a price).

Although there are many nuances that characterise the over four dozen bottled Santorini wines available, it's important to distinguish between the three main types. The *niktéri* is a dry white wine that contains 12–13 per cent alcohol by volume. This wine is at its best after it has ripened in barrels for six to seven years before bottling. A more full-bodied wine is the 15–18 per cent dry red wine *broúsko*.

The *visánto* in white, red or rosé is to be enjoyed as an aperitif. It is made from grapes sun-dried for one to two weeks before pressing and is very sweet with an alcohol level of only 8–10 per cent. Craft beer is also brewed on Santorini. You have a choice between eight varieties plus a seasonal Christmas beer, with *Yellow Donkey* and *Red Donkey* being the most popular choices.

INSIDER TIP
Island brew

AFTER-DINNER DRINKS

Some wineries still produce an exquisite grappa-like *tsípouro* by distilling the pomace left over from winemaking. As *tsípouro* is both rare and expensive, the similar drink of *rakí*, originally from Crete, is also popular on the island. Oúzo is not made on Santorini but is still often served with a meal instead of wine. The best brands in the land are *Plomarioú*, *Mini* and *Barbayánnis* from the island of Lesbos.

COFFEE AS A SCIENCE

Although most Greeks consume only a moderate amount of alcohol, they drink coffee at any time of the day. Ordering it in Greece is something of a science: first you have to choose between the traditional Greek mocha *kafés ellinikós*, the hot instant coffee generally known as *ness sestó*, and the cold, whipped instant coffee served with ice cubes, *frappé*. If you order a Greek coffee, you must always say how sweet you want it because the ground coffee is mixed with sugar and then brewed (similar to a Turkish coffee): *skétto* is without sugar; *métrio*, with a little and *glikó*, with a lot of sugar.

Greek coffee generally comes without milk. If you'd like your coffee with milk, say *mä gála*. Apart from the traditional coffee varieties, people on Santorini drink a lot of cappuccino and espresso. These are also available cold as *freddo cappuccino* and *freddo espresso*.

Wine tasting at the Venetsanos Winery

Today's specials

Starters

FÁVA SANTORÍNIS
A purée made from sun-dried yellow peas mixed with plenty of onions, vinegar or lemon juice and olive oil

CHTAPÓDI KSIDÁTO
Octopus salad marinated in vinegar and oil

TARAMÁ
A creamy reddish puree made from cured cod roe and a starchy base of white bread

Salads

CHORIÁTIKI SANTORÍNIS
A mixed salad with capers, olives, sun-dried tomatoes and féta cheese

CHÓRTA
A salad of cooked leaves of wild plants, drizzled with lemon

PATSÁRIA
Red beetroot eaten at room temperature and served with its own leaves

Meat dishes

BEKRÍ MEZÉ
Pork goulash in a slightly hot sauce with peppers

JUVÉTSI
Braised beef with baked *kritharákja* (rice-shaped barley pasta) in tomato sauce

JEMISTÉS
Large tomatoes and peppers filled with rice, minced meat and herbs

Fish dishes

BAKALJÁRO ME SKORDALJÁ
Fried dried cod with garlic-and-potato purée

KALAMÁRI JEMISTÁ
Fresh whole octopus filled with cheese

Vegetarian dishes

TOMÁTOKEFTÉDES
Balls or patties made from puréed tomatoes, onions, courgettes, flour and mint. The speciality of Santorini!

REVITHÓKEFTÉDES
Chickpea purée shaped into patties or balls and fried

BRIÁM
A type of ratatouille made from different vegetables with courgettes and aubergines

SHOPPING

SCENTS OF THE ISLAND

Santorini-born Stávros Koronéos and his daughter, who trained in Grasse on the Cote d'Azur, have created a selection of exclusive yet reasonably priced scents for the island. You can chose from three scents each for women and men, with evocative names such as Lava, Caldera and Akrotiri. They are for sale in only three shops on the island, including *Under a Fig Tree* (see p. 55) by the monastery between Imerovígli and Firostefáni. Otherwise buy online on *santorini.net*.

POTTERY FROM ANTIQUITY?

The island's potters are particularly creative, producing not just a large variety of plates, bowls, vases and other everyday objects, but also copies of antique amphoras and Minoan plates. A cluster of such workshops can be found in Mégalochóri.

ISLAND ART

Santorini landscapes are the subject of most painters on the island. Techniques range from watercolours to collages. Most of the artists' workshops are situated along the caldera-edge promenade in Oía. Leoni Schmiedel's spectacular collages are worth seeing in her workshop in Firostefáni (see p. 54).

SHOPPING FOR SPARKLERS

The cruise passengers who visit Santorini every day have attracted one jewellery shop after the other to pop up, especially in Firá. The choice is outstanding yet the prices will set you back. If you're staying on the island, don't be tempted to buy jewellery on your first day. Shop around, and if a trader notices that you're not a "one-day island hopper", he may drop the price.

INSIDER TIP Don't rush in!

You can buy pumice (right) in many shops, but you can also find it for free on the beach

CULINARY TREATS
The island's culinary specialities include the flat yellow peas used for the traditional dish of *fáva*, sun-dried tomatoes, pistachios and capers. Buy them from the producers directly at their roadside stands along the road between Akrotíri and its lighthouse.

TEXTILES
Fashion by Greek designers is a rare find in boutiques here, which are dominated by international luxury labels. The t-shirts and sweatshirts designed by the German artist Werner Hampel in Firá are an original souvenir to take back home. *Háris Cotton* in the island's capital specialises in fine cotton clothing (see p. 53).

SCULPTURES
Contemporary Greek artists exhibit their high-quality sculptures made of glass, marble and precious metals along the caldera-edge pathway in Oía and near the cathedral in Firá. There are also several stores in Oía which sell unauthorised copies of sculptures and pottery from Greek museums. Traders will send items all over the world on request for a fee.

COLLECTORS' ITEMS
Instead of buying pumice and lava in the souvenir shop, you can collect your own. Beautiful multi-coloured lava sands can be found on the White Beach in Kamári and the Red Beach in Períssa.

WINES & SPIRITS
The best place to buy wines is from one of the many wineries where you can pay to taste them first. The best schnapps is available from Antónios Argyrós at his distillery, *Art Space* (see p. 72), near Kamári which is a successful combination of gallery and winery.

SPORT & ACTIVITIES

Santorini is not famous for its sports tourism. The caldera is too small to accommodate windsurfing centres and waterskiers. The steep hillsides down to the Aegean are not suitable for large sport facilities, and the island is simply not large enough for a golf course. What's more, the tourist season lasts from June to September only, barely long enough for a water-sports centre to survive. Here, sport is a brief distraction rather than the object of a holiday – with the exception maybe of diving.

CYCLING

Santorini is not an ideal destination for longer cycling tours due to its steep gradients crammed into a small space and its mostly narrow and busy roads. One or two acceptable day tours are suitable for passionate mountain bikers. *Motor Inn (Kamári | Odos M. Aléxandrou 1 | tel. 22 86 03 11 65 | motorinn.gr)* hire mountain bikes from 12 euros per day, with electric bicycles costing from 24 euros per day. The delivery of a bike and helmet to anywhere on the island is included in the price, and can also be booked online before you even leave home. *Santorini MTB Adventures (Perívolos | Ágios Geórgios | mobile 69 80 28 94 53 | santoriniadventures.gr | from 120 euros for a half-day tour)* offer guided tours; there is an option to combine a half-day mountain bike tour from Perívolos with a half-day sailing trip on a stylish yacht from Vlicháda *(for 250 euros)*.

FISHING

Every morning at 10am and every afternoon at 3.30pm, a sizeable fishing boat leaves the Vlicháda marina for a five-hour fishing trip. In the evening, the nets are cast, and they

Whether you're in a sun lounger or an infinity pool, you can always get a view of the sea

are reeled back in in the morning. You can fish during both tours and swim in quiet coves, and the catch is later grilled and eaten al fresco. Wine and salads are provided by the crew. *Giorgaros Fishing Tours | Vlichída fishing port | tel. 69 36 71 63 48 | santorini-fishing-tours.com | morning and evening tours from 130 euros/ pers.*

HORSE RIDING

Two stables on the island offer hacks, which are also suitable for beginners. *Santorini Horseback Riding (Mégalochóri | mobile 69 89 53 04 30 | santorini-horseback-riding.com | 2-hr hack to the caldera's edge at sunset for 90 euros)* leads you around Mégalochóri and along the caldera's edge. *Santorini Horseriding (Akrotíri | mobile 69 75 54 14 47 | a 2-hr beach ride 90 euros)* takes you to the surroundings of Akrotíri and to the beach.

KAYAKING & PADDLEBOARDING

Situated on the beach in Akrotíri, *Santorini Sea Kayaking (mobile 69 51 80 10 51 | santoriniseakayak.com)* specialises in organised sea-kayaking tours. Their four- to five-hour tours along the south coast are also suitable for families with children from the age of seven *(80 euros).* The day-long tour (12 nautical miles) along the Santorini caldera to Thirasía is designed for those with kayaking experience *(225 euros).* Those who want to try their luck at stand-up paddleboarding should book a three-hour tour from Akrotíri to Vlichída and back *(70 euros).*

INSIDER TIP
Family paddling

SNORKELLING & DIVING

Snorkelling is permitted everywhere in Greece. However, if you want to scuba dive along the coast of Santorini, you need to join a tour organised daily by one of the island's certified diving centres. Such regulation aims to prevent damage to, or even theft of, the many ancient and medieval artefacts lying on the sea bed.

Diving centres offer courses for both beginners and those with experience, as well as organised dives for advanced divers. Santorini's special attraction is, of course, dives into the caldera. Tours for experienced divers cost 60 euros. Three to four-day diving courses for beginners are also available for around 420 euros, and half-day snorkelling excursions cost 30 euros. ☂ Santorini Dive Center (tel. 22 86 08 30 80 | divecenter.gr) in Eríssa; Sotirioú Diving Center (tel. 22 86 03 31 77 | scubagreece.com) in Kamári.

TENNIS

Only nine hotels on the island have their own tennis courts. Non-hotel residents can hire a court at the Santoríni Tennis Club (tel. 22 86 02 40 08 | Facebook: SantorinTennisClub) in Messariá.

TREKKING

Due to its small size, you can comfortably reach all of Santorini's resorts in a day. Although the island does not have any marked trails, footpaths or precise maps, it is difficult to get lost. However, you are often required to keep to the narrow, virtually unused paved roads due to the ever-decreasing number of unsurfaced tracks and mule paths available. On the other hand, there is a vast selection of cafés and restaurants to choose from on any hike, and a bottle of water is usually all you need to take with you.

Footwear with a good tread is an advantage because the old paved lanes and paths can be slippery. As many of the routes lack shade, headwear is recommended.

Descriptions of two interesting hikes can be found on pages 112 to 117. A number of hikes can be found free of charge at santoriniplus.net/blog/santorini-hiking. A total of 25 hikes, including precise directions, are displayed on the Santorini map (scale 1:25,000) by Anavasi publishers (anavasi.gr). The map is also available in GPS-compatible digital format.

If you don't like the idea of hiking on your own, you may want to join one of four five-hour guided hikes offered by Santorini Walking Tours (Firostefáni | caldera-edge pathway | tel. 22 86 03 64 96 | santoriniwalkingtours.com | 85 euros/pers.). Groups have a maximum of six participants, and hotel transfer is included in the price.

WINDSURFING & KITESURFING

There are two surf centres on the beaches of the shallow east coast: Monólithos Beach is home to kite specialist Santorini Kite (mobile 69 44 53 92 62 | santorinikite.gr | 2-hr lessons for 180 euros). Windsurfers on the island gather at the Nemely Center (Kamári | Odós Avís | mobile 69 39 31 51 27 | nemelycenter.com | 1-hr lessons for 45 euros, 5 hrs for 179 euros) in the northern part of Kamári Beach. Both businesses hire sports equipment.

Other water-sport centres specialise in high-speed activities, hiring out jet skis and speed boats. Here you can be suspended in the air as you parasail behind a motor boat, go water skiing or wakeboarding, or enjoy a peaceful time in a pedal boat or sea kayak. On the southern end of Períssa Beach is the water-sports centre *Wave Sports (on Perívolos Beach next to Beachclub Chilli | tel. 22 86 08 10 90 | wavesports.gr).*

YACHT CHARTER

Bareboat charters cannot be hired on Santorini, but chartered yachts are available all over the island – especially for exclusive day cruises around the caldera. The website *santorini.com/sailing* offers a good selection of motor boats and sailing yachts in different sizes. Expect to spend at least 800 euros for four people for a day tour.

Windsurfing on the east coast

Hiking with a view: on the track from Pýrgos to Ancient Thera

REGIONAL
OVERVIEW

E g

Art galleries, small
harbours and
fabulous sunsets

PERÍSSA & THE SOUTH p. 80

An ancient town,
trendy beaches
and unspoilt nature

2 km
1.24 mi

o Pelagos

OÍA & THE NORTH p. 96

Oía

Ormos Mousaki

FIRÁ & AROUND p. 38

FIRÁ

A dazzlingly white
settlement right at the
caldera's edge

KAMÁRI & THE CENTRE p. 58

Ormos Balos

Kamári

Beaches, wineries
and antique ruins

Períssa

*Kritiko
Pelagos*

FIRÁ &
AROUND

This is a dream come true. You will have seen this fantastic scenery in countless photos, calendars and TV ads. Now you are actually standing by the caldera's edge, and it is a breathtaking sight. There is no other view in the world quite like this!

From Firá, your gaze takes you into the caldera and far across the Aegean Sea. Sit on café and restaurant terraces or low walls and feel as if you are on a heavenly balcony. Walk the narrow lanes, full of shops and life, and ride on the cable car towards the anchored cruise

When the sun sets on the horizon off Firá, the restaurant terraces fill up

liners and yachts. Perhaps you are staying in an incredible hotel perched on the crater's edge between sky and volcanic rock. And if you want to know more about this spectacular place, you can visit some of the interesting museums and learn about the 5,000-year history of the island. Later on, explore the nightlife in pubs and clubs under a starry sky. You can catch up on your sleep the next day on the nearby beaches.

FIRÁ & AROUND

MARCO POLO HIGHLIGHTS

★ **PREHISTORIC MUSEUM**
Sensational finds from the Akrotíri ruins
➤ p. 43

★ **ORTHODOX CATHEDRAL**
An insight into the Greek soul ➤ p. 44

★ **CATHOLIC DISTRICT
(TA FRÁNGIKA)**
A sea of tranquillity between churches
and monasteries in Firá's oldest quarter
➤ p. 46

★ **CABLE CAR**
A steep ascent towards the caldera
➤ p. 47

★ **VOLKAN ON THE ROCKS**
Best view and delicious food ➤ p. 52

★ **MÁTI ART GALLERY**
Fish depicted alone or in shoals made of
bronze, moulded glass, steel and iron
➤ p. 54

Ceramic Art Studio

Volkan on the Rocks ★

7 Skála (Old Port)

100 m
109 yd

‖ Símos

10 Skáros Rock

8 Ágios Nikólaos Convent
‖ Under a Fig Tree
‖ Mýlos

25ης Μαρτίου

25is Martiou

9 Kontochóri Folklore Museum

Agiou

Athanasiou

Ghízi Museum
(Mégaron Ghízi)
4
‖ Kapári
5 Catholic District (Ta Frángika) ★
6 Cable Car ★

3 Archaeological Museum

Agiou

Athanasiou

▽ White Doors

‖ Nikólas

Diónysos in Atlantis ‖ ‖ ‖ Enigma Club

New Art 🛍 ‖ Murphy's

Kirá Thíra ▽

Háris Cotton 🛍

‖ Fu Li Hua

Danezi M Δανέζι
‖ Stamná ‖ Lukumum

Café Classico ▽ ▽ Two Brothers

Koukoumávlos ‖

Lalaoúnis 🛍 AK Gallery

Máti Art Gallery ★ 🛍

Orthodox Cathedral ★ 2

Agiou

Athanasiou

Agiou

1 Prehistoric Museum ★

Náoussa ‖

Mitropoleos Street

🛍 Kyrá Níki

🛍 Leoni Schmiedel

The path to Firostefáni

FIRÁ

(⫟ E–F4) **With a population of 1,850, Firá is the seat of the island's administration. The town sprawls into the villages of Firostefáni and Imerovígli, as well as the inland village of Kontochóri. These were once independent communities but have now been incorporated into the town.**

Many cruise-ship tourists do not have the time or interest to venture beyond the old town limits of Firá, which makes the main streets very crowded when they're around in summer. Firostefáni and Imerovígli are just as beautiful as Firá but far quieter. While all three parts of the town offer tavernas, fine restaurants and adventurous hotels hewn into the caldera cliffs, Firá has a much more vibrant nightlife than its little sisters.

SIGHTSEEING

Are you planning to spend a day visiting museums? You will need at least five hours to take a comprehensive journey through 5,000 years of Santorini's history in the capital's museums. The best place to start is the *Prehistoric Museum,* housed in a modern building directly opposite the central bus station. It documents the island's earliest history up to around 1600 BCE. On leaving this museum, take a stroll around the Firá of today until you reach the *Archaeological Museum,* which picks up precisely from where the Prehistoric Museum left you.

After discovering about Firá up to the time of Jesus' birth, head to the *Orthodox Cathedral* to learn more about the religion actively practised in Greece for the last 2,000 years. Your tour through history continues at the *Ghízi Museum,* where you can explore the period of Roman Catholic domination on the island, as well as depictions of the last volcanic eruption and photos of the 1956 earthquake.

Finish your museum tour in the *Kontochóri Folklore Museum* on the edge of Firá, and learn how the islanders used to live in the 19th and 20th centuries before the arrival of mass tourism.

1 PREHISTORIC MUSEUM ★

Some things are really worth knowing. This – the most entertaining museum on the island – will let you become immersed in an age when, while northern European hunters and gatherers still lived in caves, Santorini was home to Europe's first advanced civilisation. The museum mainly houses finds excavated from Akrotíri since 1976; this was the site of a catastrophic volcanic eruption around 1600 BCE. The museum trail takes you anticlockwise around the museum. The boards exhibited in room B are very informative, focusing on Santorini's geology and history (in both Greek and English). A cabinet on your right displays ancient fossils of plants and animals found in the lava, including fossilised olive tree leaves dating back 60,000 years.

The next wall cabinet contains Cycladic idols (mainly female figurines) from around 2800–2400 BCE. Their characteristic features include the flat head with long nose, the long almost phallus-shaped neck, the breast and groin outlines and crossed arms pressed against the chest. The large 3D model of the Akrotíri excavation site is worth a closer look. If you haven't visited Akrotíri yet, it provides you with a first impression of the urban character of this settlement which flourished between 1700 and 1600 BCE.

INSIDER TIP
Understanding Akrotíri

The next rooms contain archaeologists' collections that reveal how well the people lived and organised their community in past times. The cabinet

directly behind the 3D model of Akrotíri exhibits plaster casts of fossils found in volcanic ash, including a wooden chair, a three-legged table, a mobile clay oven and two long, dog-shaped sets of barbecue supports for grilling meat skewers, similar to today's *souvláki*. Surprisingly, a bath tub is another of the museum's artefacts. Cabinets exhibiting weights and other objects provide evidence that the people of Akrotíri developed an ingenious system of measurement.

The second part of the museum tour is dedicated to the world-famous Akrotíri murals, and starts by explaining the technique involved. Various bowls are on display filled with colour pigments and 3,700 year-old limestone remains. Not only were the walls painted in Akrotíri, but many other smaller objects were ornately decorated too, such as a house altar designed as a three-legged table and painted with dolphins.

The last room in the museum presents two frescoes from the 17th century BCE, one depicting an unknown four-legged mammal and the second depicting eight cavorting monkeys. This fresco of monkeys clearly shows the freedom of expression enjoyed by painters of this time: each monkey is different, with seven painted in profile and one front-on.

The last artwork on display was only discovered in Akrotíri on 12 December, 1999: a golden goat ("goat idol") dating to the 17th century BCE. This is a sensational find, not only because of its unique beauty but because the inhabitants of Akrotíri took most of their precious metal with them when they fled from the imminent volcanic eruption. It also offers hope of finding other such works, as 97 per cent of the Akrotíri settlement has yet to be excavated by the archaeologists. *Opposite the main bus terminal | Apr–Oct Wed–Mon 8.30am–4pm, Nov–Mar 8am–3pm | admission 3 euros | ⏱ 30–45 mins*

2 ORTHODOX CATHEDRAL ★ 🕆

Perching on the caldera edge in Firá, this snow-white building with prominent bell tower is one of the island's landmarks and visible from far. It was built as recently as 1956/57, after the old Orthodox Cathedral from 1827 had been destroyed by the 1956 earthquake. The cathedral's interior is immediately spectacular, with valuable crystal chandeliers and an artistic iconostasis. The most eye-catching artworks are the cathedral's paintings, which stretch over the interior walls and ceilings. They are the work of Christóforos Asímis, a painter born in Éxo Goniá on Santorini in 1945 who still lives on the island today. The paintings were funded by the island's Orthodox community. The cathedral is dedicated to the Feast of the Purification of the Blessed Virgin Mary (Candlemas), and if you take time to study the paintings, you will come closer to understanding the Orthodox religion and its religious art.

Start by gazing at the paintings above you in the dome. It is the highest point of the church and symbolically represents heaven. This is why the dome in Orthodox churches always depicts Christ as *Pantokrátoras*, the Almighty. As in nearly every Orthodox place of worship, the Four Evangelists can be found in the dome's pendentives. They represent the transition from the dome's heavenly sphere to the church's earthly setting, indeed people only learnt about the appearance of Christ through the Gospels.

Now take a look in front of you towards the iconostasis. Above this display of icons (which separates the church from the altar space) you will see a depiction of the Annunciation. The Archangel Gabriel is visible on the left, rushing to announce to Mary that she will give birth to God's son – the start of Jesus's life on earth. His end is portrayed nearby in the painting of the Ascension on the underside of the altar arch. The various stages in the life and suffering of Jesus are depicted on other frescoes inside the church. Mary's life is also the subject of a series of paintings in the apse. *Caldera-edge pathway | daily from sunrise to sunset | free admission | ⏱ 10–15 mins*

3 ARCHAEOLOGICAL MUSEUM

If you don't like museums much, you can safely skip this one, although you may feel intrigued by the many small objects that inform us about life 2,500 years ago. The tour starts in the ticket entrance hall which exhibits prehistoric objects found on the island before excavation began in Akrotíri. Three particularly beautiful specimens include the tiny clay pots displayed at the top of the glass cabinet you pass

Biblical history is told through the mosaics and paintings in Firá's Orthodox Cathedral

on entering the large hall. They are known as the nipple pots and, if you look closely, you can see why.

Walking around the large hall in a clockwise direction, your tour will start with one of the museum's main treasures in the wall cabinet on your left. This solitary object of a well-preserved clay statuette dates to the second half of the 7th century BCE. Standing just 30cm / 1ft tall, it depicts a lady tearing her hair out in grief, a common ritual practised even today in Greece and also by the mourners in the cult film *Zorba the Greek*.

A 7th-century BCE clay storage vessel decorated with ornate reliefs stands at the back of the hall on your left. In the centre of the hall stand the remains of two sculptures depicting nude male youths, so-called *koúroi* (pronounced: *kúri*). Free-stone statues such as these were erected across the

Aegean islands in the 7th century BCE, during the Archaic period in Greece, usually in sanctuaries to honour the God Apollo. The sculpture of the youth that is preserved from his crown to thigh indicates that the original statue was colossal in size. The following wall cabinets display a lot of painted pottery from the 8th and 7th century BCE, with a splendid bear in the first free-standing cabinet after the *koúroi*.

The two clay vessels on display in the cabinets when you enter the smaller side room are worth seeing: ancient war ships are painted on the inside with a clear image of a naval ram on the ship's bow, a generously painted captain, and, on closer look, the heads of the rowers.

The last free-standing cabinet in the side room contains a clay drinking vessel from the Hellenistic period showing a rather explicit depiction of a horned satyr, from the troop of male companions of the God Dionysus, sitting on a horse with a belly full of wine. Dionysos was the God of wine and fertility, which explains why the satyr is depicted with an overly large erection. *At the northern end of the caldera-edge pathway near the cable car station | Apr–Oct Wed–Mon 8.30am–4pm, Nov–Mar 8am–3pm | admission 2 euros | ⏱ 15–30 mins*

4 GHÍZI MUSEUM (MÉGARON GHÍZI)

Housed in a Venetian building dating from around 1700, which was once the home of the well-established Ghízi family, this museum is now in the hands of the Roman Catholic Church. It is only worth a visit if you have a keen interest in the Catholic Church. If not, just take a peek into the museum's pretty courtyard.

The museum exhibits contracts, wills, letters and manuscripts belonging to the Church since around 1550, as well as historic maps of Santorini and the other Cycladic islands. Colourful engravings and prints show islanders dressed in traditional costume, as well as the island's villages and natural beauty.

The first floor houses contemporary Greek and international art from painters living on Santorini or others who have explored the island. *Odós Eríthrou Stavroú (signposted from the cable car and Archaeological Museum) | May–Oct Mon–Sat 10am–4pm | admission 3 euros | ⏱ 10–20 mins*

5 CATHOLIC DISTRICT (TA FRÁNGIKA) ★

The district known as Ta Frángika, or "The Frankish", is situated immediately to the east of the cable car top station in

Spectacular ride: take the cable car from the village to Firá's port

the main town. From the early 18th century, this district was home to most of the Roman Catholics (known colloquially as the Frankish) who remained on the island after the end of the Italian rule. The district's main architectural attractions are the *Domincan Convent* and the *Roman Catholic Cathedral*; these are situated in the street nestled between the cable car station and the *Mégaron Ghízi museum*.

The difference between the tiny Catholic convent church and an Orthodox Church is striking on entering: it features a font, confessional box and above all religious statues. The Dominican nuns who reside in the convent come from all different countries, and they warmly welcome visitors to their services *(daily 6.15am, 7.45am, 12.15pm, 4.10pm, 6pm, 7.30pm, 9pm and 1am)*. The church is always open.

Just a few doors down on the opposite side of the street stands the small Roman Catholic Cathedral, which dates from 1823 and is dedicated to John the Baptist. *Services on Sat 7pm, Sun 10am and 7pm | church doors always open to the public in the daytime | ⏱ 10 mins*

6 CABLE CAR ★ 👥

If you are lucky and there is only a short queue of cruise-ship tourists at the cable station, take the opportunity and enjoy a great ride into the crater and the old harbour of Skála.

Since the early 1980s, two sets of six connected cable cars have connected Firá to its old port, transporting passengers up 225m / 738ft in just two minutes. Manufactured in Austria, the cable car was donated by shipowner Evángelos Nómikos, who was born on the island; it is now in the possession of the community. *Cable car top station on the caldera edge next to the Archaeological Museum (well signposted) | daily 6.30am 9pm, until later in high summer | single ticket 5 euros*

7 SKÁLA (OLD PORT)

Have you any energy left? A wide, cobblestone path with 587 steps connects the caldera-edge promenade in the main town of Firá to its old port which the locals refer to as *skála* (as many ferry terminals in Greece are called). Where fishing boats and freight carriers once docked is now the port of call for cruise-ship passengers who are transported back and forth from their luxury liners to the dock. Dozens of

The Folklore Museum: embark on a journey through time to Santorini in 1900

mules and their operators are waiting to carry guests up to the main town (a 15-minute ride). The path between Firá and Skála is well trodden by the animals and, if on foot, be careful not to be run over by a mule or stand in their droppings. It's worth walking down the cliff on foot – after all, you can always take the cable car back up. There are cafés, tavernas (€€) and souvenir shops selling cheap stuff tailored to the tourist market.

8 ÁGIOS NIKÓLAOS CONVENT

Two friendly nuns live in Santorini's last inhabited Orthodox convent. Although the convent dates from 1674, the convent's church was only built in 1820. The gates are always closed but will be happily opened to those interested in a visit at visiting times (just pull the rope to ring the bell). The many votive tablets hanging on the icon of Saint Nicholas indicate that the patron saint of sailors, fishermen and children works many wonders on Santorini. *Imerovígli, at the north end of the caldera-edge pathway | daily 8am–12.30pm, Jun–Sep also 4–7pm | l free admission | ⏱ 10 mins*

INSIDER TIP
Please ring!

9 KONTOCHÓRI FOLKLORE MUSEUM

In this museum you will get personal attention. Emanuíl Lignós' private museum is an homage to how locals used to live and work on the island in the 19th and early 20th century. It includes a cave cellar hewn 35m / 115ft into the pumice rock, which was mainly used to store wine and food as well as a traditionally furnished cave dwelling. An old carpenter's workshop, blacksmith's and a shoemaker and cooper's workshop have also been recreated. The first floor houses a library with a large collection of books on Santorini and old tourist brochures and guides. *Kontochóri, below the road between Firá and Oía | May–Oct daily 10am–2pm | admission 3 euros | ⊙ 30 mins*

⑩ SKÁROS ROCK

Below the village of Imerovígli, a striking lava-layered rocky mound stretches out into the crater, visible from many spots on the caldera's edge. This marks the spot of the island's capital during the Venetian period from 1207 to the middle of the 16th century. Worldly rulers, as well as the island's Roman Catholic bishops, all had their castles built here. Due to its precarious position on crumbly stone however, the Turks chose to abandon this settlement. In 1811, its last inhabitants moved to Imerovígli and newly founded Firá, leaving castles and buildings behind to rot. The 1956 earthquake inflicted even greater damage on the settlement, so what remains today is almost nothing.

Anyone with a head for heights and adventure can climb the Skáros rock. Take the path leading from the Blue Note restaurant at the panoramic viewpoint of *Ágios Geórgios Chapel* downwards over the ridge and then up to the Skáros peak. If you're really brave, you can continue to the tiny *Agía Theosképasti Chapel* which clings to the rock on the other side of the mound. *Imerovígli | open to the public, the chapel is closed | ⊙ 1 hr*

INSIDER TIP
Scared of heights?

THE MULES OF SANTORINI

A mule ride from the old port up to the main town of Firá is an exciting way for cruise tourists to kick off their tour of the island. Forty operators own a total of almost 400 mules with which they earn their money in the busy summer months. Every morning, they lead the mules from their stables on the edge of town down to the port and back again in the evenings. The work is just as hard for the operators as it is for their four-legged companions. Their earnings are supplemented by the shares they own in the cable car, which amount to 20 per cent of the profits made. Although animal lovers question the working conditions of the mules, the operators insist that they are well taken care of (santorini-donkeyunion.com). "Donkey Republic" is an art project that has been contributed to by artists from all over the world, who have created brightly coloured donkeys and mules from fibreglass and which are now on exhibition in public spaces. Smaller replicas are available as souvenirs. A share of the proceeds is donated to the SAWA mule and animal sanctuary near Karterádos.

EATING & DRINKING

DIÓNYSOS IN ATLANTIS

Relatively cheap taverna despite its central location. Features a large terrace, though without view of the sea and caldera. Traditional plain style interior and Greek food without any fuss. Its main attraction is its excellent selection of traditional Greek *tsípouro*, a spirit made from various types of grapes. *Odós Er. Stavroú, near cable car station | tel. 22 86 02 38 45 | daily from noon | €€*

INSIDER TIP
Delicious spirits

FU LI HUA

Absolutely authentic Chinese food – hence the great number of Chinese tourists you will encounter here! Apart from various soups, poultry and pork, the restaurant also serves tripe and pig's feet. Chinese spirits (58 per cent alcohol!) are only available by the bottle. *By the Food Plaza in the northern part of the platía | tel. 22 86 02 26 99 | daily 11.30am–11.30pm | €*

KAPÁRI

On a delightful terrace, behind a cascade of flowering bougainvillea, owner Kóstas serves up creative Greek and Santorini specialities without charging extra for the caldera view. The restaurant serves bread with caper butter and Cretan pomace brandy. Try one of the various Santorini tomato creations, the chicken in an ouzo-and-honey sauce and lamb in vine leaves. *Approx. 300m / 984ft from the platía on the road to Firostefáni | tel. 22 86 02 70 86 | santorinikapari.gr | Apr–Jun daily from 2pm, Jul–Oct daily from 4pm | €–€€*

KOUKOUMÁVLOS

Hewed into the caldera cliff, this stylish gourmet eatery was one of only three restaurants on the Aegean islands to repeatedly win the "Toque d'Or", a prize awarded by Greece's leading restaurant guide. The owner and master chef Níkos Pouliásis uses mainly regional ingredients, and creativity reigns to conjure up dishes such as risotto flavoured with Greek coffee, or traditional fáva yellow pea puree combined with a smoked eel and passion fruit mousse. It is advisable to book ahead by phone. *Caldera-edge pathway opposite the Orthodox Cathedral | tel. 22 86 02 38 07 | koukoumavlos.gr | daily from 7pm | €€€*

KYRÁ NÍKI

If you're prepared to miss out on the caldera view, you'll be treated to freshly made Greek cuisine at prices accepted by most locals. You can choose many of the dishes directly at the counter. The excellent salad comes served in an edible bowl made of a hard cheese from the island of Náxos. A popular lunchtime haunt of local business people and civil servants. *800m / 2,625ft from the bus station on the road to the airport | tel. 22 86 02 51 46 | Mon–Sat from noon to 10pm | €–€€*

LUKUMUM

Greeks enjoy late-night snacks and preferably something sweet. One speciality is *loukoumádes*, deep fried

Winds of change in an old mill: modern cuisine in Mýlos

pastries with sesame, cinnamon and honey or filled with chocolate, walnuts and candied cherries or even served with ice cream. Sit outside on bar stools at old casks that serve as tables. In *the lane which starts at the northern end of the platía | daily from 7.30am | €*

MÝLOS 🍴
An ideal destination, especially on bad weather days thanks to its conservatory built on three sides of a renovated round windmill. Located directly on the caldera edge, the panoramic view is accompanied by contemporary Greek and fusion cuisine; a six-course tasting menu is also available. The chef is always pleased to accommodate vegetarians. *Caldera-edge pathway at Firostefáni | tel. 22 86 02 56 40 | mylossantorini. com | daily from 5.30pm | €€*

NÁOUSSA 🍴
It is no wonder that patrons are queuing up for this renowned taverna – most of them holding a glass of ouzo or another drink. Yet its prices remained affordable so you can enjoy the view without paying a fortune. The owners from Macedonia serve the finest Greek taverna food with a spicy Macedonian touch. *Caldera-edge*

pathway below the Orthodox Cathedral | tel. 22 86 02 12 77 | naoussa-restaurant.com | daily from noon | €€

NIKÓLAS

One of the capital's oldest eateries, this tiny, virtually windowless taverna with no outdoor seating consciously resists any form of change. The menu is limited to a small selection of traditional dishes. The queues outside the restaurant are testimony to the quality of the food. No table reservations accepted. *Odós Er. Stavroú, near the platía in Firá | all year round, daily from noon | €€*

SÍMOS ⚑

A classic taverna with no view over the caldera but with excellent food. Instead of ordering a main evening meal, you can put together a traditional Greek *mesé* from a selection of small dishes. The waiter will carry over a tray of dishes for you to choose from, which he will then serve to your table. *Firostefáni, left on the main road from Firá to Imerovígli | tel. 22 86 02 38 15 | tavernasimos.gr | May–Oct daily from noon, Nov–Apr daily from 5pm | €-€€*

INSIDER TIP Eat like the Greeks

STAMNÁ 🍖

From early morning, chickens, gyros and other meat is being grilled in the entrance of this taverna, which opens out onto the busy street. The display counter features always the same dishes: *moussaká* and *juvétsi*, *pastítsio* and green beans. The rustic

salad is always freshly prepared, the *zaziki* is home-made. Perfectly good food, albeit nothing special, but the eight staff who work the half-open room like busy bees are quite spell-binding. From their second visit, patrons are greeted with a handshake. Ouzo and fruit are served after after a meal, as per an ancient Greek custom and should always be on the house, although this is becoming increasingly rare on Santorini these days. *In the lane which leads downhill from the northern end of the platía | tel. 22 86 02 18 60 | daily from 11am | €*

INSIDER TIP Ouzo on the house

VOLKAN ON THE ROCKS ★

This is arguably the deli with the most picturesque location in Europe. Sit on a large shady terrace directly above the caldera to have the best view of the slightly lower-lying Firá and Profítis Ilías. You can brunch until 4pm and enjoy all kinds of delicious snacks from the whole of Greece. The menu includes excellent cheese, sausage and fish boards with exclusively Greek produce, many being suitable for vegetarians, as well as ice cream, cakes and cocktails. You may want to spend an entire day here eating and soaking up the atmosphere. Fresh vegetables, cheese, sausages and much more are also available to take away. *By the caldera-edge pathway below the Nómikos Conference Centre | tel. 22 86 02 83 60 | daily from 9am | €-€€*

INSIDER TIP Order the platter

SHOPPING

AK GALLERY

Here, the island painter Christóforos Asímis, creator of the murals in the Orthodox Cathedral next door, sells his watercolours, which feature mainly scenes from Santorini. You can also buy exquisite jewellery and sculptures made by his partner Eléni Kolaítou-Asimís. *Fabrica Shopping Center on the caldera-edge pathway*

and bowls he creates. *Near the caldera-edge pathway, near the Nómikos Conference Centre*

HÁRIS COTTON

Trendy fashion for women and men featuring high-quality cotton at affordable prices, which is the key to the success of the en-vogue Greek retail chain. *Central Square | hariscotton.com/stores/santorini*

Sculptures show the way to Máti Art Gallery next to the Orthodox Cathedral

CERAMIC ART STUDIO

The Santorini-born potter Andréas Alefrákis exhibits his works for sale in his pottery studio. He combines aspects of traditional Greek pottery with the Japanese technique of raku in the objects, candle holders, vases

LALAOÚNIS

Greece's most famous jeweller, Ilias Lalaoúnis, has stores worldwide and even his own jewellery museum in Athens. On Santorini, Lalaoúnis is of course present in a central location. It's worth getting a sneak preview of

Take the bus to Períssa Beach

the typical style of the master online or in the store window. *Caldera-edge pathway, near the Orthodox Cathedral | iliaslalaounis.eu*

LEONI SCHMIEDEL

Since emigrating from Germany in 1997, this artist has become renowned for her unique collages, in which she incorporates items she finds on the beach and in nature (such as lava sand and Santorini volcanic ash), as well as old account books and letters. The colours she uses reflect the shades of Santorini. Visitors are welcome in her workshop on the caldera edge.

Firostefáni | signposted from the church square on the caldera edge

MÁTI ART GALLERY ★

Founded in 1989, this unique gallery is the brainchild of the sculptor Yórgos Kýpris and the Greek group of artists known as "Studio 71". Fish are Yórgos Kýpris' favourite subject, and are portrayed as the victims of human consumption, e.g. a plate of bones or squashed into cans. They are available as aesthetic sculptures, wall pieces, free objects, jewellery pendants and more. The artist works with the same materials – mainly bronze and glass, as well as steel and iron – he uses for the boats he creates. *Fábrika Shopping Centre next to the Orthodox Cathedral | matiartgallery.com*

NEW ART
The artist Werner Hampel transforms t-shirts, sweats and hoodies into works of art. He prints them with his own designs, producing new creations every year. He likes using well-known and enigmatic symbols, icons and lettering in his graphic designs; the "walking man" is his trademark. *Fabrica Shopping Center on the caldera-edge pathway*

UNDER A FIG TREE
Are you looking for that special souvenir? This small boutique is a treasure trove of rare Santorini scents by *Santorini Paysages*, which are only produced in small quantities but are still affordable. The shop also sells fashion and accessories exclusively by Greek manufacturers. *Imerovígli, on the footpath below Ágios Nikólaos Monastery*

INSIDER TIP
The scent of Santorini

SPORT & ACTIVITIES

ÁNEMOS
The old port of Skála is home to the fast Ánemos speedboat which can accommodate up to 12 passengers. It is available for charter and caldera cruises. *Skála, mooring in front of Nikólas snack bar | tel. 22 86 02 29 32 | santonet.gr/sailing/anemosboat | approx. 130 euros / hr, minimum 2 hrs*

BEACHES

If you are staying in Firá, Firostefáni or Imerovígli, the closest you get to a swim is in your hotel or complex pool. The pool of the campsite on the lower edge of the village is open to the public, provided you order a drink at the bar.

However, the bus service is an efficient, quick and affordable way of reaching many of the island's beaches, for example in *Kamári*, *Monólithos*, *Períssa* and *Perívolos*.

WELLNESS

DR. FISH
Walking through Firá can be quite hard on the feet. Why not give them a rest and have a treatment that involves small fish nibbling the hard skin off your feet.

All the while you can watch life on the *platía* go by. *Platía | tel. 22 86 02 35 63 | 5 mins 10 euros, 30 mins 15 euros*

ENTERTAINMENT

CAFÉ CLASSICO
Come here for the sunset and stay for hours. The bar is spread over several small terraces perched on the caldera edge with amazing views.

Enjoy the sunset with international music playing in the background; later on in the evening you're more likely to hear Greek music. Be prepared for steep prices. *Caldera-edge pathway near the Orthodox Cathedral |santoriniclassico.gr | daily from 9am*

ENIGMA CLUB

This disco has been a popular haunt for Greek and international tourists alike for over 30 years. The place is tightly packed with people; clubbers dance in the spacious whitewashed interior and, before midnight, in its courtyard and terrace. *50m / 164ft from the platía in Firá, on the left along the road to Oía | daily from 11pm*

KIRÁ THÍRA

This small bar plays mainly jazz. The artistic interior was designed by the amiable owner, Dimítrios Tsavdarídis, himself. Even the frescoes depicting Greeks drinking in Ancient Thera are his creation, as are the sculptures around the bar. The bar's trademark drink is sangria made with Santorini wine. *Odós Erithroú Stavroú | daily from 8pm*

MURPHY'S

This pub is open round the clock, and transforms into one of the island's clubbing and dancing hotspots in the evening. British and Irish guests are often caught dancing on the pub's long bar. Some of the evening's special moments are caught on camera and posted on the pin board for everyone to see on the morning after. *Odós Georgíou D. Nómikou | murphys barsantorini.eu | daily from noon*

TWO BROTHERS 🐖

This bar is where staff from restaurants, cafés and tavernas meet after midnight when they have finished work. That's why between 9pm and midnight you can enjoy drinks at happy-hour prices: every second one is free! But drinks here are very affordable anyway, and you can also try blowing smoke rings with the hookah. *Parallel lane above the platía | 2brothersbarsantorini.com | daily from 10am*

THE WHITE DOOR

If you like somewhat cheesy entertainment, this is the place for you. Every evening, for a hefty price tag, you can partake in the Greek Wedding Show. By the end of the event, there is Greek dancing for all and smashing of plates on the dance floor in the good old traditional way – all accompanied by snacks and as much wine as you can drink. *Odós Er. Stavroú | whitdoorsantorini.com | daily 9–11pm | 55 euros*

AROUND FIRÁ

VOURVOÚLOS

Platía in Vourvoúlos approx. 3km / 1.9 miles from Firá, 10 mins by car
Vourvoúlos is one of the villages on Santorini built into a gorge where cave dwellings and houses have been sculpted out of the steep valley walls. Take a stroll along the old village road through the precariously steep valley and you will notice that most of these cave dwellings are now only used for storage or keeping animals.

The bus stop is on the main road from Firá to Oía. From here, a narrow, steep path takes you down to the village's main square where you can also park up. The village square houses the

Homes of the dead: funerary chapels in Vourvoúlos look like a village in bloom

Ágios Efstáthios Church (which is normally closed) and a typical war memorial. From this *plátia*, take the steep road to Áno Vourvoúlos and up the Firá–Oía road for approx. 100m / 330ft until you reach the 🚩 *village cemetery* on your left which is worth visiting; it contains 13 replica tiny chapels with mini blue domes built for the village's more prosperous families. The graves of the less affluent inhabitants are located on the churchyard in front. 🕮 *F3*

ÉXO GIALÓS
4km / 2.5 miles from the plátia in Firá, 10 mins by car
This tiny coastal settlement is relatively unknown to tourists as is its dark lava sand beach which runs along the coast until it merges with the beach in Monólithos; although there is no

sunshade or lounger hire, you will have the beach very much to yourself. 🕮 *G4*

KARTERÁDOS
1.5km / 1 mile from the plátia in Firá, 5 mins by bus
You won't find any cruise-ship passengers in Karterádos, and will be able to enjoy this typical Santorini village on foot. Dilapidated cave dwellings and Classicist villas are an indication of the wide range of social distinctions that already existed in earlier centuries. The eye-catching *Ágios Christódoulos Church* offers wonderful views of the three gorges in which the village was built. The parish also includes the 350-m / 1,150-ft *Karterádos Beach* of coarse volcanic sand and lava. The volcanic scenery is great for photographs but not particularly suitable for bathing. 🕐 *1 hr* | 🕮 *F4*

KAMÁRI & THE CENTRE

A CLASSIC BEACH HOLIDAY

Kamári is the classic seaside resort on the island. The beach promenade is a pedestrian zone, and the 5km / 3 miles of lava sand and shingle stretch from the airport to the steep cliffs of Mésa Vounó, on top of which you find Ancient Thera, a settlement from the 1st century BCE that has been excavated by archaeologists.

Firá and the caldera edge are within easy reach by bus until late at night, and prices in Kamári are significantly cheaper than up on the

A splash of yellow next to the typical white and blue: belfry in Mégalochóri

clifftop. Tourists in the village come from all over the world, and noise levels from the nearby airport are very low. A number of destinations can easily be accessed by bicycle, including several wineries. The relatively unspoilt hinterland offers some beautiful villages. The view of the open Aegean Sea and across to the small island of Anáfi is a delightful alternative to the expensive caldera view, and the whole of Santorini can be seen from the peak of Profítis Ilías.

KAMÁRI & THE CENTRE

erados
τεράδος

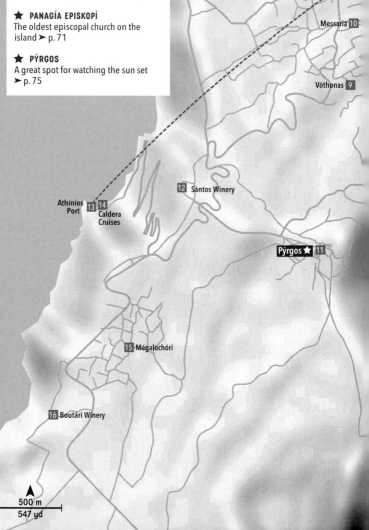

MARCO POLO HIGHLIGHTS

★ **CÍNE KAMÁRI**
The latest films and premium sound under a Mediterranean moon ➤ p. 66

★ **ANCIENT THERA**
Excavations high above the sea ➤ p. 69

★ **PANAGÍA EPISKOPÍ**
The oldest episcopal church on the island ➤ p. 71

★ **PÝRGOS**
A great spot for watching the sun set ➤ p. 75

Messariã 10

Vóthonas 9

12 Sántos Winery

Athínios Port 13 14
Caldera Cruises

Pýrgos ★ 11

15 Mégalochóri

16 Boutári Winery

▲
500 m
547 yd

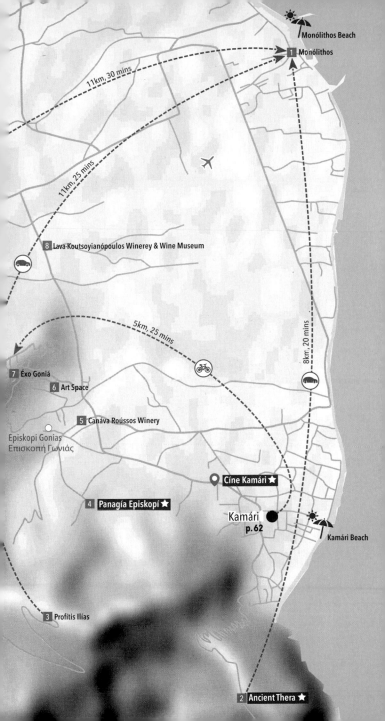

Monólithos Beach

1 Monólithos

11km, 30 mins

11km, 25 mins

8 Lava-Koutsoyianópoulos Winerey & Wine Museum

5km, 25 mins

8km, 20 mins

7 Éxo Goniá

6 Art Space

5 Canáva Roússos Winery

Episkopi Gonias
Επισκοπή Γωνιάς

Cíne Kamári ★

4 Panagía Episkopí ★

Kamári
p.62

Kamári Beach

3 Profítis Ilías

2 Ancient Thera ★

KAMÁRI

(G–H6) **Only 40 years ago, Kamári (pop. 1,400) was the only resort on Santorini to attract a handful of holidaymakers. The old promenade stretched from what is today the restaurant Iríni to the Hotel Kamári Beach, in those days the only hotel in town.**

Today, Kamári has the most hotels, B&Bs, tavernas and bars along the east coast. The village's old centre has disappeared, replaced by a landscape of new buildings along the flat coastline, increasingly also stretching inland up to Profítis Ilías. The dark Kamári Beach starts directly beneath the steep cliffs of Mésa Vounó and spreads north to Monólithos.

SIGHTSEEING

BEACH PROMENADE
In Kamári, virtually the entire holiday will focus on the 5-km / 3-mile beach and the 1.2-km / 0.75-mile pedestrianised beach promenade that runs immediately behind it. If you are not sun-bathing or swimming, you will likely be people-watching as they walk up and down the promenade from a café or taverna. And some visitors might find that this is actually more interesting than visiting endless old stones and tiny chapels ...

ÁGIOS NIKÓLAOS CHAPEL
Anyone who is on holiday in Kamári will at some point walk up to this tiny chapel. Of no particular architectural or historical importance, it perches on a prominent cliff edge above the south end of the beach at the foot of Mésa Vounó and offers splendid views of Kamári. The chapel itself is closed to the public. The tiny cave nearby was used as a customs post in the 19th and early 20th century, while some of the smaller caves were home to devout hermits in the 17th and 18th centuries.

CLIFFS OF MÉSA VOUNÓ
What a rock! The best way to explore the rugged and mighty beauty of Mésa Vounó is by taking a short 15-minute boat ride from Kamári to Veríssa or vice versa. The tiny boat "Eléni" will take you up close to the steep cliffs, but be warned; the sea's currents can cause the boat to rock even though the waters appear calm. It is best to wear shorts because in Kamári the boat cannot moor and you will need to wade through the shallow water. **INSIDER TIP Shorts recommended** *Departs approx. every hour between 8am and 5pm from the beach in Kamári, arrives in Veríssa at the north end of the beach | single journey 5 euros*

EATING & DRINKING

AMALTHÍA
This taverna attracts tourists with plentiful seating in its decorative garden and on the flower-filled terrace, as well as friendly, cheerful and efficient service and a wide selection of food. Its *kléftiko* is delicious, a lamb stew

KAMÁRI

Cíne Kamári ★

Μεσαριά - Καμάρι

Appolonos

Απόλλωνος

Galíni Appolonos

Makedonias Μακεδονίας

Monólithos Beach

Kantína o Minás

Panagias Παναγίας

Myrtidiotissas Μυρτιδιώτισσας

Cíne Villaggio

Blanc du Nil

Beach promenade

Groove Bar

Prince

Vasileos Thira

Μακεδονίας

Νυμφών

Kamári Beach

Jutta's Café

Club Albatross

Μακεδονίας

Nymfon

Amalthía

Salíveros

Archaías Thiras Αρχαίας Θήρας

Νυμφών Nymfon

Irini

Hook Bar

Cliffs of Mésa Vounó

Agios Nikólaos

200 m
218 yd

cooked in the oven together with spices, onions, vegetables, cheese and potatoes wrapped in baking paper and aluminium foil. *On the main road inland in the south of the town | tel. 22 86 03 27 80 | daily from 10am | €€*

GALÍNI 😾

Away from the tourist hustle, this taverna (called "cheerful serenity") invites guests onto its beachside terrace. Literally just 10m / 30ft from the

Aegean, it seats up to 80 guests. The main highlight on the menu is fresh fish. The catch of the day is displayed on the counter, and often includes the small, shiny fish which the locals call *paximádia* – a deep-fried, white-fleshed fish with few fish bones.

INSIDER TIP
Delicious fish platter

On cooler evenings you can sit inside the lava walls hung with fishing nets. On a clear night, with no artificial light around, the sky lights up. During the day, parents can stay seated on the terrace while their young ones play on the beach in front. *Agía Paraskeví Beach, 3km / 1.8 miles to the north of Kamári | tel. 22 86 03 29 24 | galiisantorini.gr | daily from noon | €€*

IRÍNI

A nostalgic place. Opened in 1965, this is Kamári's oldest taverna. Despite a new building built round the old one, it has retained much of its charm. This is mainly thanks to Iríni, its chirpy, old owner with the sun hat, who is proud to show guests her signature book full of famous personalities. The main attraction though is the diverse menu with fresh fish and Santorini specialities. *On the southern end of the promenade | tel. 22 86 03 12 46 | daily from 8am | €€*

JUTTA'S CAFÉ

This café has a delightful, lovingly decorated garden terrace. It is run by Berlin-born owner Jutta, who emigrated to Santorini in 1967. Jutta serves German sausages with potato salad, cask beer and delicious homemade cakes with good coffee. Background music and a relaxed setting all attract guests to this small oasis away from the tourist hustle. *Tavli* boards and dice shakers are available for guests. *Odós Vasiléos Thíras (on the outer main road) | tel. 22 86 03 19 54 | daily 9am–6pm, in high summer until 9pm | €*

INSIDER TIP
Take it easy

KANTÍNA O MINÁS 🐷

This very simple taverna serves food from the grill until 4am. The menu includes small chicken or pork skewers and gyros as well as – on Wednesdays and Saturdays – roast suckling pig, the meat being ordered by weight. It is a place preferred by ordinary Greek people because the taverna has the lowest prices in the entire village. *In the village centre between Odós Apollónos and Odós Panagías Mrytitiótissas | tel. 28 86 03 28 39 | daily from noon | €*

PRINCE

The Prince is a sassy modern restaurant, which also serves snacks to those on loungers on the beach. The island's traditional yellow pea puree *fáva* is served here flavoured with caramelized almonds, and the red, sweet-paprika *florinís* are filled with cheese from central Greece and fresh onions. A favourite with locals is the "prince pork fillet", stuffed with Cypriot halloumi cheese and plums. *Centre of the promenade | tel. 22 86 03 31 22 | princesantorini.com | daily from noon | €€*

SALÍVEROS

One of the resort's oldest tavernas and decorated with traditional Greek furnishings: blue wooden chairs with woven seats and chequered tablecloths. The mother-of-three owner, Maroulía, and husband, Pétros, whose main job is as a criminal investigator, serve the finest traditional food. Their children and nephews all help with the service. Many of the vegetables

Jutta's Café offers German fare on a beautiful terrace

are home-grown; the olive oil comes from Pétros' olive trees in Crete. *Almost at the southern end of the promenade | tel. 22 86 03 17 02 | daily from 10am | €€*

SHOPPING

BLANC DU NIL

This cool shop sells nothing but white outfits for women and men, all made of premium Egyptian cotton and the height of fashion. *At the final bus stop*

SPORT & ACTIVITIES

KAMÁRI BEACH WATERSPORTS

The place for adrenalin junkies. The company doesn't just hire jet skis, but also offers extreme high-speed tours: one via jet ski from Kamári to the volcanic islands in the caldera *(⏱ 2½ hrs | 300 euros/pers.)* and another tour around the entire island *(⏱ approx. 3½ hrs | 500 euros/pers.)*. Those who prefer to be chauffeured can circumnavigate the island on a speedboat with a pilot *(⏱ approx. 3½ hrs | 500 euros/boat, max. 4 passengers).* What they offer for water skiing and wakeboarding is more conventional. Sea kayaks and stand-up paddleboards can also be hired. *North end of the beach | tel. 69 76 93 63 24 | santorini-watersports.gr | May–Sep*

BEACHES

KAMÁRI BEACH 🏄

This long stretch of dark sandy and pebbly beach (5km / 3 miles) is only populated with sun loungers and parasols in the resort's centre and in front of the hotels in the north. Those looking for a more secluded spot to bathe should head further north. There is also a water sports centre *(see p. 65)* at the north end of the promenade. ⊞ *H6*

MONÓLITHOS BEACH 🏄 ⛱

Up to 30m / 98ft wide and 1,400m / 5,000ft long, this dark lava sand and pebble beach has a shallow slope making it the best beach on the entire island for children and inexperienced swimmers. The tamarisks dotted along the beach provide natural shade. There are sun loungers and parasols for hire, a beach volleyball court and a large, imaginative play area for children in the centre of the beach. ⊞ *G4*

> **INSIDER TIP**
> **No big waves**

WELLNESS

BEACH MASSAGE

The entire beach in front of the promenade is served by massage therapists, predominantly from East Asia. You may want to watch first how they are working on someone else's back before asking for a treatment yourself. *Approx. 25 euros/30 mins*

ENTERTAINMENT

CÍNE KAMÁRI ★

The open-air Ata in Kamári is an iconic summer venue, combining state-of-the-art Dolby Surround technology with a traditional garden setting complete with an open-air bar serving drinks and snacks. Movies are shown in their original language with Greek subtitles. *Mamma Mia!*, the blockbuster starring Meryl Streep and the Abba soundtrack, is a continuous hit. Tickets can be booked online or by phone. *Situated on the main road to Kamári on entering the resort | tel. 22 86 03 34 52 | santorinicinema.com | end of May–beginning of Oct, daily 9.30pm | admission 8 euros*

CÍNE VILLAGGIO

Open all year round, this air-conditioned cinema in the modern shopping centre specializes in English language films. *Odós Vasiléos Thirá | tel. 22 86 03 28 00 | villaggiocinema. gr | several showings a day | admission 8 euros, or 5 euros 🎭 on special cinema days (usually Tue / Wed)*

CLUB ALBATROSS

The place to meet up on the promenade in the evening for a relaxing drink on its sea-view terrace under small palm and tamarisk trees. After midnight, guests move indoors to party on into the night and dance a

At Cíne Kamári the projector runs every day in summer

syrtáki. Promenade between Odós Zafiropoúlos and Odós Mégas Aléxandros | daily from 7pm

GROOVE BAR

Typical British pub which attracts sports fans with its large screen TVs showing sporting events, beer fans with its international selection of 60 ales and lagers, and music lovers with songs from the 1960s to '80s, reggae, rock 'n' roll, and even sometimes live acts. *Odós Vass. Filíppou | daily from noon*

HOOK BAR

Very popular bar playing mainly old-ies but goodies. Wide choice of cocktails. *On the promenade to the south of Odós Mégas Aléxandros*

AROUND KAMÁRI

1 MONÓLITHOS

5km / 3 miles from Kamári, 20 mins by bicycle

This tiny coastal settlement was named after a monolith, an imposing 33-m / 108-ft high limestone rock which towers above the airport plateau. Dating back 200 million years, this rock is, like the mountains of Profítis Ilías and Mésa Vounó, what remains of the island's pre-volcanic past. To the south of the rock, the white *Chapel of Ágios Ioánnis* overlooks the airport's runway. The village houses are scattered over the hillside, and chimneys belonging to old tomato paste factories dominate the coastline. One of these factories is still in operation for a brief period during summer. Nestling between the factories is an electricity plant which produces the island's power, and even a small hotel

shelters you from sand storms when the wind is strong. From here, the remains of the old pier, from where the factories would ship their tomato products, can be seen jutting out into the sea. A tiny port to the south does little to conjure up images of a roman-

Location, location, location!
This mantra appears to have been true even at the time of Ancient Thera

has been squeezed in between the industrial buildings.

Highly rated among many locals is the *Taverna Skaramángas (tel. 22 86 03 17 50 | daily | €€),* with its tables and chairs set out on the edge of the car park next to one of the tomato paste factories; their *kakaviá* (fish soup) is excellent, but only available on pre-order. Just a few steps further south is the *Kapetán Loízos (daily | €€),* another taverna offering the same quality and prices as Skaramángas, but in a large, spacious interior which

tic fishing village.

The tiny coastal road heading north from Monólithos offers a bizarre landscape to your left and right, first passing by old, desolate cave dwellings followed by strangely shaped pumice stone walls covered in graffiti. On closer observation and with a little imagination, you may believe you can decipher Chinese lettering, chiselled out by the wind and waves.
G–H4

INSIDER TIP
Chinese carvings?

2 ANCIENT THERA ★

2.7km / 1.6 miles from Kamári on a switchback road, 45 mins on foot

The impressive headland of Mésa Vounó lies between Kamári and Períssa, and its cliffs plunge into the Aegean. The island's main settlement was situated on a ridge of this mountain for over a thousand years. Between 1886 and 1902, the German Baron Hiller von Gärtringen used his own funds to excavate the site, digging 6m / 20ft deep into the layers of volcanic ash. Excavation work was taken up again between 1990 and 1994 by a team of archaeologists from Berlin. EU funding was then used to make the entire site accessible to the public, with explanatory boards as a guide for visitors.

Even if you're not interested in antiquity, the 45–60-minute walk, or a car or mule ride, is well worth the journey to stroll through the sparse ancient ruins in a unique, lonely landscape of natural beauty at a dizzying height.

The ancient city of Thera was founded around 1000 BCE by Doric colonists from the Greek mainland. Most of the building remains, however, date from the Hellenistic period, when the south Aegean Islands were under the rule of the Ptolemaic dynasty in Egypt. They turned Santorini into an important naval base. Ancient Thera lost its importance in Roman times and was completely abandoned in the 7th century under Byzantine rule.

The tiny *Ágios Stéfanos Chapel* is at the entrance to the site and stands on the remains of an early Christian basilica. Built on a foundation of ancient stones, the multi-coloured lava walls of the chapel are now threatening to collapse. The remnants of antique pillars perch on top of barrel vault roofs. A fragile wooden door lets you have a look inside the chapel.

Continue along the side of the ridge that faces Kamári and you will reach the *Témenos of Artemidóros*. Artemidóros, a Ptolemaic admiral, had this shrine built in honour of several Gods. In the rock you will see

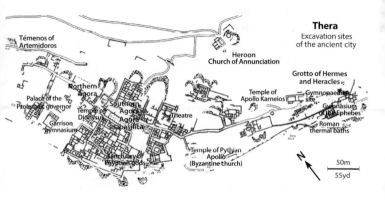

Thera
Excavation sites of the ancient city

What about a selfie with the church bells at the peak of Profítis Ilías?

engravings of an eagle to symbolise Zeus, king of all gods, a lion for the honoured God Apollo, a dolphin for Poseidon and a portrait of Artemidóros himself.

The path then takes you to the ancient *agorá*, the main market square which is 100m / 330ft long but surprisingly narrow. Take a rest on one of the modern benches under the wind-sheltered trees. In the centre of the *agora*, steps lead up to what is left of a temple in honour of the god Dionysus, the ancient god of wine, theatre and religious ecstasy. The relief at the foot of the staircase is also dedicated to Dinoysus. It depicts two rings which are supposed to be testicles – maybe it used to signpost the way to a Roman brothel. You are now standing on one

INSIDER TIP
A subtle hint?

of the nicest spots of this ancient city, overlooking the remains of the ancient *theatre* from the 2nd century BCE. The theatre was large enough to seat 1,500 people, and the entire hollow space underneath was used as a cistern.

The path continues to the spur of the mountain ridge but is sometimes closed to the public. If open, you will reach a large *cliff terrace*, which in Doric times was a religious cult site where boys would dance naked at *gymnopaediae* to honour Apollo. Festival guests would engrave the names of some of the boys into the rocks next to the names of the various Gods. The oldest examples of this *graffiti* date from the 7th century BCE.

The entrance to the *Temple of Apollo* from the 6th century BCE can also be accessed from this terrace.

Inside you will see a small gate building leading to a courtyard which was the original site of this temple. It had a flat roof and was divided into an antechamber and a main room, the *cella*, where the icon of the god is located.

This sacred area also enclosed a *grotto* dedicated to Hermes (Roman: Mercury), the god of trade and thieves, and Heracles (Roman: Hercules), the legendary ancestor of all Dorians.

A path leads from the theatre over the peak of Mésa Vounó to the Períssa side of the hill. You first pass the sanctuary of the Egyptian Gods dating from the 2nd century BCE. The niches hewn from the rock contained gifts to the gods and their statues stood on a platform carved out of the rock. You will then pass a well-preserved *cistern*, the foundations of the *Palace of the Ptolemaic* governor and the *gymnasium* where the wrestlers in the Ptolemaic garrison would train. *Wed–Mon 8.30am–2.30pm | admission 4 euros, ☛ admission free Nov–Mar on 1st Sun of each month*

If you're driving, a narrow, roughly paved zig-zag road takes you from Kamári to Ancient Thera. A *mini-bus* service also runs to Ancient Thera *(single 10 euros; return 15 euros)* and departs from the junction between the road to Ancient Thera and the main road in Kamári. Departure times: *hourly 9am–2pm.* Tickets are available both at the bus stop and from *Ancient Thira Tours (on the bypass shortly before its beach-facing end) | tel. 22 86 03 24 74 | ancient-thira.gr | ⊙ 1–2 hrs |* ⊞ *G7*

❸ PROFÍTIS ILÍAS
12km / 7 miles from Kamári,
25 mins by car

A zig-zag tarmac road leads you up from Pýrgos to the island's highest mountain (567m / 1860ft). Despite its narrow size and hairpin bends, many excursion coaches still take this road. Although you are treated to a spectacular panorama of Santorini and the Aegean, the view of the summit itself leaves you disappointed as the monastery at the top is surrounded by a dozen antenna masts.

Founded at the start of the 18th century, the *monastery* stands directly below the summit and its present construction dates back to 1852–57. Like many of Greece's monasteries and churches on mountain tops, the monastery is dedicated to the prophet Elias who, according to the Old Testament, ascends from a mountain up to heaven on a chariot of fire. The monastery is closed to visitors, but the *monastery church* is open for certain services *(Wed, Fri, Sat 4–5.30pm, Sat also 6–8.30am, Sun 4.30–8.30am only).*

The new chapel *Ágios Nektários,* which is located below the entrance to the monastery, is always open to the public and features pretty domes and half-domes adorned with traditional roof shingles. ⊞ *G6–7*

❹ PANAGÍA EPISKOPÍ CHURCH ★
5km / 3 miles from Kamári,
25 mins by bicycle

The "All Saints Episcopal Church" is one of the island's oldest and most interesting churches. The building was commissioned by a Byzantine Emperor in 1115 and was the island's Byzantine cathedral until 1207; it has been a listed building since 1962. Also known as the *Panagía Goniás*, the church is surrounded by an unspoilt landscape and a pretty churchyard with flowerpots, cypress trees and a carob tree.

At the site of the church, prior to its construction, there was an ancient shrine, elements of which have been incorporated into the church building, including the ancient pillars and their capitals (the topmost member of the pillars). The apse is divided by filigree pillars and capitals from the late antiquity period. *Entrance from the road between Firá and Kamári, signposted from Mésa Goniá | daily 10am–noon and 2–5pm | donations welcome |* ◷ *20–30 mins |* ▭ *G6*

▣ CANÁVA ROÚSSOS WINERY
4km / 2.5 miles from Kamári,
10 mins by bicycle
Founded in 1836, the island's oldest winery is now a museum and a romantic location for wine-tasting, with the wine being produced elsewhere in a modern winery. On the vine-covered, lava-wall terrace, guests are invited to taste wines accompanied by a plate of traditional Santorini specialities (*romanparadosiakó santorinió piáto*). *Southwest of the road between Kamári and Messariá on the outskirts of Mésa Goniá, at the turn-off to the Panagía Episkopí church | canavaroussos.gr | daily 11am–7pm | wine-tasting (5 glasses) 15 euros |* ◷ *20–30 mins |* ▭ *G6*

▣ ART SPACE
2km / 1.2 mile from Kamári,
10 mins by bicycle
Located on the outskirts of the village of Éxo Goniá, Antónios Argyrós has converted this old winery into one of Europe's most atmospheric art galleries. He exhibits work by contemporary artists in the old wine caverns between mid-April and the end of October. The prices for these paintings vary from 200 euros to well into the five-figure range.

The gallery owner speaks fluent English and enjoys showing visitors around the exhibition himself; he provides plenty of background on the artists, as well as the winery's history and its old equipment. One of the cellar rooms originally housed a large cistern while another was used as the stable. These rooms still contain many historic artefacts that tell the island's history, from the production of tomato paste and distilling of spirits to wine pressing. Visitors are treated to a unique experience without any obligation to buy anything or pay an admission fee.

What is more, the owner Antónios has started to produce his own wine and distil spirits in the old caverns, reviving the old winemaking tradition. You will be invited to taste and, of course, buy his products at the end of the tour. This is the best wine-tasting experience on Santorini away from the caldera and cruise-ship tourists – there are strictly no coach tours organised to this winery. *Well signposted from the main road between Messariá and Kamári; bus stop on the*

The lovingly designed wine museum at Lava-Koutsoyianópoulos Winery

main road (from there 300m / 1,000ft on foot), | tel. 22 86 03 27 74 | artspace-santorini.com | daily 11am –sunset | ⏱ 45 mins | ▥ G6

7 ÉXO GONIÁ

3km / 1.9 miles from Kamári,
5 mins by car

This village spreads out over the hillside to the west of the road linking Kamári to Messariá. On the outskirts of the village, along the road to Pýrgos, stands the landmark church of *Ágios Charálambos* (closed to the public), a building notable for its redtiled roof rather than a traditional Hellenic blue dome. Its forecourt is adorned with geometric mosaics made from multi-coloured lava rock.
▥ F–G 5–6

8 LAVA-KOUTSOYIANÓPOULOS WINERY ☂ & WINE MUSEUM

5km / 3 miles from Kamári,
20 mins by bicycle

The island's largest privately-owned winery has been producing wine since 1880, and wine producer Geórgios Koutsoyianópoulos has opened a small wine museum in his old wine cellar. The museum exhibits winemaking artefacts, such as old goat hides once used to transport wine, wine barrels that can hold up to 3,000 litres and various wine presses, as well as distillation vessels for producing spirits. Eighty years of Santorini winemaking history is illustrated using old photos and nice dioramas. *30m / 100ft east of the road from Kamári to Messariá (well signposted)* |

Sunset and storm clouds: a dramatic setting at Pýrgos

volcanwines.gr | Jun–Oct daily 10am –7pm, Apr/May/Nov daily 10am–5pm, Dec–Mar Mon–Sat 9.30am–2pm | museum visit with wine-tasting (4 glasses) 11 euros | ⊙ 1 hr | ⊞ G5

🔟 VÓTHONAS

7km / 4 miles from Kamári, 15 mins by car

Vóthonas is a quiet village relatively undisturbed by tourism and well-preserved for the authenticity-seeking visitor. You will not find a coffee shop or taverna here. The village is hidden from view along the road between Kamári and Messariá, and only comes into brief view on the road between Messariá and Pýrgos. That's because Vóthonas lies in one of Santorini's traditionally narrow gorges, with many of its buildings carved out of the gorge's walls while the rest perch precariously on the steep hill. The place is almost completely uninhabited; most of the cave dwellings now serve as stables or storage facilities only. You can reach Vóthonas by taking the narrow concrete road (almost free of traffic) signposted from the road between Kamári-Messariá opposite the *Kritikós* taverna *(tel. 22 86 03 23 00 | daily from noon | €)*, which serves fresh BBQ meat. ⊞ *F5*

🔟 MESSARIÁ

4 km / 2.5 miles from Kamári, 5 mins by bus

Nearly every tourist to Santorini passes through Messariá once during their stay; the village (pop. 1,075) stands at the island's most important junction where the road to the airport and Kamári diverts off from the road to Pýrgos and Akrotíri. Despite its unappealing setting, this crossroads has become the village square, full of tavernas, cafés and stores. If you head 200m / 650ft away from the crossroads, past the playground, sports ground and a large cistern, you will be treated to the beauty of old Messariá. You will discover the *Village Church of Ágios Dimítrios,* with its unrendered walls exposing the red, black and grey lava, and the remains of two industrial tomato paste factories. Built in neoclassical architectural style in 1888, the two-storey mansion *Archontikó Argyroú* reveals in what splendour the Santorini winemaker and wine merchant Georgios E. Argyrós and his family lived 100 years ago *(diagonally opposite the village school on the main square | argyrosmansion.com | May–Oct Tue, Wed, Fri–Sun 10am–6pm | admission 5 euros).* ☐ F5

⑪ PÝRGOS ★

8km / 5 miles from Kamári,
15 mins by car

Pýrgos is the island's highest village at 350m / 1148ft. Its old centre is dramatically situated on a high hill and, in Venetian times, was a fortified settlement with a small castle at its highest point. During the Turkish occupation, it advanced to become the island's capital. It's well worth taking a trip to Pýrgos any time of day, but particularly for the sunset, which is just as spectacular here as it is in Oía but without the crowds. Open after sunset, the wine bar and gourmet restaurant *Selene (1 min from the square*

INSIDER TIP
Peaceful sunset

on your left above the road to the *Profítis Ilías Monastery | tel. 22 86 02 22 49 | selene.gr | restaurant open daily noon–4pm and from 7pm, wine bar open daily 5pm–midnight | €€€)* is rated as one of Greece's best and most expensive restaurants. The restaurant offers creative Greek and Mediterranean cuisine, while the wine bar serves sweet homemade pastries from their own patisserie or a cheese board with nine different Greek cheese specialities to accompany their great-tasting wines.

The bus stops at the village square, which forms the heart of the village with a few shops, a kiosk and a handful of bars. Two alleys lead up from the *platía* to the *Kástro district,* which you enter through an alleyway tunnelled under a house. The first building you pass is the Christós church (closed to the public). Penélopi and her husband Mános (who resembles Aléxis Zorbás from the famous film) own the traditional *Penelope trattoria (daily | €)* which serves bites to eat. It is worth trying the *tomatokeftédes,* homemade wine and, for dessert, figs and grapes marinated in syrup.

From the Christós church, it is only 200m / 650ft to the highest point in the Kástro district. To get there, walk round the church, unfortunately also closed to the public. You will come to a *bastion* offering fantastic views of the island, the airport and the Kástro district with its church domes, bell towers and crosses. Between June and September, it's worth visiting the village's small icon collection *(usually Tue–Sun 10.30am–3pm | free admission),* with works from the 17th and 18th century from various churches in the region. ▢ *F6*

⓬ SÁNTOS WINERY

*8km / 5 miles from Kamári,
15 mins by car*

The winery belonging to Santorini's cooperative of 800 winegrowers is a large, tourist-focused complex in a splendid caldera-edge setting. Its wine-tasting shop, where you can also buy gourmet local products, resembles a supermarket rather than a cosy wine bar and is often overrun with tourists. *50m / 160ft to the east of the road from Firá to Akrotíri at the junction to Pýrgos | santowines.gr | open daily 10am–sunset | wine-tasting 18.50 euros for five glasses and 35.50 euros for 10 glasses | ⊙ 30–40 mins | ▢ F6*

⓭ ATHÍNIOS PORT

*10km / 6 miles from Kamári,
20 mins by taxi*

The island's ferry terminal and trade port lies directly below the steep caldera edge, with a well-paved, zig-zag road leading you up the caldera cliff-side (300m / 984ft) and to the main road running between Firá and the island's south. The long harbour (150m / 492ft) is lined with tavernas, cafés, travel agencies and car rental firms. The port is a hive of indescribable activity during the summer months when the ships dock and sail off – a must-see, especially for those who have travelled to Santorini by plane.

A circle of orange buoys to the north east marks the point where the Cypriot *Sea Diamond* cruise liner ran aground in 2007 and eventually sunk just 300m / 984ft off the coast. Despite the risk of oil pollution, the wreck has never been raised because the Greek government, the cruise line operator and the insurers cannot come to an agreement about who is to pay for what. ▢ *E6*

⓮ CALDERA CRUISES

A cruise through Santorini's caldera by boat is one of the most memorable holiday experiences on the island. Boats usually set sail from the Athínios

BY BOAT AND BUS

The island's travel agencies organise trips around the island every day. For example, you can book a day tour that visits Profítis Ilías, the Akrotíri excavations, the lighthouse at the tip of Akrotíri, Perívolos beach and a winery. This type of tour costs around 40 euros excluding admission fees. A half-day coach tour takes you from Kamári to Panagía Episkopí on to Pýrgos, with an evening sunset at Oía (35 euros). Full-day boat tours around the caldera cost 40 euros, including a bus pick-up from your hotel; boat trips from Kamári to one of the beaches near Akrotíri plus a beach barbecue cost 45 euros.

port (others from the old port in Firá or from the Arméni port in Oía). Tours depart several times a day with a pick-up from your hotel and last approximately four hours. Information is available from all tour operators or travel agencies and directly at the ports.

Most tours visit three different spots in the caldera. The first anchor is at the active volcanic island of *Néa Kaméni* created by a volcanic eruption in the early 18th century). The last lava

and 1941). On the gravel path up the crater, you will pass smaller craters, which erupted between 1926 and 1941, and notice the incredible colours of lava rock – yellow from sulphur, reddish brown from iron and red from manganese. Steam rises up from the small vents in this deserted lava outcrop, which stands in surreal contrast to the snow-white houses along Santorini's caldera edge. Hard to believe that vegetation actually grows on Néa Kaméni, yet the island has

Hot spot: caldera boat tours stop on the lava island of Néa Kaméni

eruption was recorded in 1950, yet even today white vapours rise from the island's many sulphur vents. Although the air smells of rotten eggs, it is completely harmless. The boats dock in the bay at Petroulioú from where it will take you 25 minutes to reach the top of the 124-m / 407-ft high volcanic crater, Ágios Geórgios (formed by eruptions between 1939

over 150 species of plants including mint, sage, rockrose and kermes oak.

Your second port of call is *Paléa Kaméni,* which erupted from the caldera around 197 BCE, and further volcanic activity over the years has changed its size and shape. The sea water in this bay is heated by thermal springs (30–40°C) and you can swim in the water which is brown from the

sulphur and iron. Remove any watches

and jewellery before swimming, because the mineral waters will discolour precious metals in a matter of seconds.

The third stop on the cruise is the tiny port of Korfós on Thirasía, an island inhabited by only 150 people. Bathe in the clear water on the narrow pebbly beach, or grab a bite to eat and drink in one of the island's tavernas.

15 MÉGALOCHÓRI

*9km / 5.5 miles from Kamári,
15 mins by car*

Although Mégalochóri translates as "large village", the name has lost its meaning today since it is one of the island's smaller communities with a population of only 460. This pretty village is worth visiting, especially in the morning or late afternoon, for its narrow lanes, traditional houses and many churches (closed to the public).

From the bus stop (at the car park furthest south of Mégalochóri), follow the paved road for 150m / 490ft into the village's historic centre. The entrance to the village is marked by a passageway running underneath the bell tower of the *Church of Iésódia tis Panagías* (dedicated to the Presentation of the Blessed Virgin Mary). If you are one of the lucky few to find the church doors open, you will notice that the walls inside are covered in traditional Byzantine frescoes.

The village square is situated directly in front of the church; take 290 paces along the main street and you will reach the three-storey belfry, which also bridges the street. If you follow the steps behind the tower, you will arrive at the square in front of the *Church of Ágii Anárgiri*. As its name suggests, the church is dedicated to the "Silverless" or "Unmercenaries" – two physicians who treated the sick and accepted no payment for their services. The doctors' names are inscribed on the church's bell towers: Cosmas and Damian.

Well signposted from the square is the ✈ *Winery Gaválas* just 150m / 490ft away. Both admission and wine-tasting in the secluded courtyard are free of charge *(tel. 22 86 08 25 52 | gavalaswines.gr | daily in high summer 10am–8pm, otherwise until 5.30pm)*.

A few paces above the winery is the *Symposion by La Ponta (well signposted in the village | tel. 22 86 08 53 74 | symposionsantorini.com | May–Oct Tue–Sun 10am–10pm, Mar / Apr, Oct 10am–7pm)*, a cultural project that is unique in the whole of Greece – it is dedicated to antique Greek music and its instruments. There are 45-minute guided tours *(Tue–Sun noon and 4pm | admission 10 euros)* which introduce you to 15 antique instruments. On three evenings each week *(Tue, Thu, Fri)* hour-long concerts are held; the shop sells Greek flutes and bagpipes that are handmade by the project. Alternatively, you can take part in an hour-long workshop and make your own antique flute *(booking required | 20 euros)*. The project also has a botanical garden with plants

A stroll through Mégalochóri will lead you past churches, belfries and walled courtyards

from ancient Greece, as well as a wine café where wine is served in the custom of Homer's age.

Mégalochóri also offers good shopping facilities along the bypass road to Períssa and Akrotíri, where seven 🏺 workshops sell creations by painters and ceramicists. Dimítris Béllos and Aspasía Vóvola produce high-quality copies of antique art at their *Art Centre Akrón (akron-art.gr)*, with life-size replicas of the frescoes from Akrotíri (some measuring up to 1.8m / 6ft). They also paint vases and other ceramic jugs in the style of the Minoan period, geometric period and Greek classicism, and also lay mosaics. If you continue along the main road to Akrotíri, you will pass the workshop *Michalisk*, owned by the painter *Michális Karamolégos*, who specialises in Santorini landscapes without any element of kitsch. Next door stands *Galatéa's Pottery Studio (galateaspottery.eu)*, exhibiting contemporary ceramic items as well as works inspired by prehistoric Akrotíri. 🕮 *E–F6*

16 BOUTÁRI WINERY

10km / 6.2 miles from Kamári, 20 mins by car

The company Boutári is one of Greece's major wine producers, with its headquarters in Náoussa, Macedonia, northern Greece. Do not expect a one-to-one guide or personal wine-tasting session here. The audio-visual show is very well organised though and guided tours are available in English. *250m / 820ft to the west of the main road from Pýrgos to Akrotíri, on the right-hand side when you leave Mégalochóri to the south (follow the sign)* | *boutariwinerysantorini.gr* | *main opening times daily 10am–4pm, May–Sep 10am–7pm, closed Jan/Feb* | *wine-tasting (5 glasses) plus guided tour 15 euros* | 🕙 *30–45 mins* | 🕮 *E6*

PERÍSSA & THE SOUTH

The southern part of the island, between the long, sandy beach of Períssa and Cape Akrotíri with its lighthouse, is the wildest part of Santorini and remains dominated by agriculture. This is the preferred area for those who like to explore as well as for lovers of fabulous beach bars.

Some of the beaches are not yet connected by paved roads, and are only accessible via tracks, with the track to the only beach directly by the caldera being breathtakingly steep. In contrast, the wide

The lighthouse signals to ships from Cape Akrotíri at the southwestern tip of the island

beaches of coarse sand at Veríssa and Perívolos are packed with pre-dominantly Greek holidaymakers on sun loungers, and many clubs open as soon as the sun sets. Sightseeing includes not just the unique excavations at 3,500-year old Akrotíri, but also a former tomato-paste factory which is now a cultural centre. Those who long for peace and tranquillity can hike to the lighthouse or one of the many windmill ruins of Emborió – arguably the quietest and most unspoilt of all villages on the island.

PERÍSSA & THE SOUTH

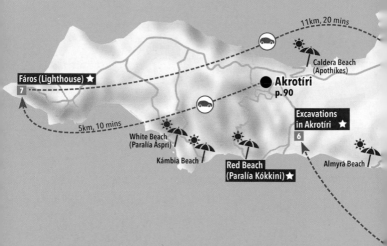

11km, 20 mins

Fáros (Lighthouse) ★
7

Caldera Beach
(Apothíkes)

● Akrotíri
p. 90

Excavations
in Akrotíri ★
6

5km, 10 mins

White Beach
(Paralía Áspri)

Kámbia Beach

Red Beach
(Paralía Kókkini) ★

Almyrá Beach

MARCO POLO HIGHLIGHTS

★ **EMBORIÓ**
A quiet and as yet unspoilt village ➤ p. 86

★ **NÓTOS THERME & SPA**
Wellness in the caves of a former ice
factory ➤ p. 89

★ **RED BEACH (PARALÍA KÓKKINI)**
A red lava beach at the bottom of bright
red cliffs ➤ p. 93

★ **EXCAVATIONS IN AKROTÍRI**
The remains of Europe's oldest city ➤ p. 93

★ **FÁROS (LIGHTHOUSE)**
Wild cape with far-reaching views ➤ p. 95

Mesaria
Μεσαριά

Vothonas
Βόθωνας

Exo Gonia
Έξω Γωνιά

Agia Paraskevi
Αγία Παρασκευή

14km, 20 mins

Pyrgos Kallistis
Πύργος Καλλίστης

Episkopi Gonias
Επισκοπή Γωνιάς

Kamari
Καμάρι

Megalochori
Μεγαλοχώρι

2 Ancient Thera

1 Panagía tis
Katefiánis

3 Emborió ★

● **Períssa**
p. 84

4 Perívolos

5 Vlichada

Agios Georgios
Άγιος Γεώργιος

Nótos Therme & Spa ★

Exomitis
Εξωμύτης

14km, 25 mins

1 km

0.62 mi

PERÍSSA

(□ G7) **After Kamári, Períssa (pop. 500) is the second-largest coastal resort on the island. While Kamári is awash with package tourists, Períssa is popular with young Greek socialites and backpackers.**

The town does not have an historic centre as such; daily life takes place along the 4-km / 2.5-mile long *beach road*, which pedestrians share with cars and scooters, and which is lined with cafés, tavernas and beach clubs.

SIGHTSEEING

AGÍA IRÍNI
The little of what remains of the early Christian Agía Iríni basilica (also *Agía Eiríni*) from the 5th/6th century is evidence that Períssa was once an ancient settlement. Other wall remains were excavated along the road to Emborió close to the *platía*. The basilica ruins are closed to the public due to danger of collapse. *30m / 100ft inland at the north end of the beach*

EATING & DRINKING

DEMILMAR
Here you can spend the entire day and half the night as well. The large and entirely white beach restaurant is on the rocky cape that separates Períssa from Akrotíri. The menu is vast, offering pizza and pasta, risotto and paella, steak or lobster. Champagne can be ordered by the glass, or vodka and gin also by the bottle. You will be waited

PERÍSSA

Agía Iríni — Demilmar

Tony's Art Gallery

Pèrissa Porto Castello

Waves Chill Out

Μεγαλοχώρι - Περίσσα

Yazz

Megalochori - Perissa

God's Garden

Ntomatíni

Lava

Tranquilo Bar

200 m
218 yd

upon on your sun lounger until midnight and a DJ plays popular songs during the day. *At the northern end of the beach | tel. 22 86 08 59 70 | daily from 9am | €€–€€€*

GOD'S GARDEN 🐷
Although the restaurant's green terrace lies directly on the main road, the delicious and affordable Santorini food and efficient service more than make up for its unspectacular setting. *On the left of the main road to Emborió | tel. 22 86 08 30 27 | daily from 11am | €*

LÁVA
Taverna with tables under tamarisks. The owner, Ioánnis, invites guests into the kitchen to look inside the pots before ordering. Also serves good vegetarian dishes and excellent house wines. *At the southern end of the beach | tel. 69 75 74 06 47 | daily from noon | €*

NTOMATÍNI
The young couple who own the restaurant like to re-interpret old Greek and Cretan recipes. Their sausages and smoked pork are shipped over from Greece's largest island and their fish soup with fresh vegetables – only available on pre-order – is renowned. *At southern end of port road | tel. 22 86 08 30 15 | ntomatini.com | daily from 10am | €€*

INSIDER TIP
Tasty soups

PÈRISSA PORTO CASTELLO
Located on the main promenade, this relaxed taverna with unique rooftop garden appeals to your average holidaymaker in search of good value for money rather than a fine-dining experience. The restaurant offers several 🐷 affordable tourist specials and the menu is spiced up with Lebanese specialities. *At the northern end of the port road | tel. 22 86 08 28 29 | daily from 10am | €–€€*

SHOPPING

TONY'S ART GALLERY
Carpenter and hotelier Antónios Prékas dedicates his free time to art and produces original collages of Santorini landscapes from lava, pumice stone and volcanic ash on old wood in traditional island colours. *To the right of the main road to Emborió | daily 9–11pm*

SPORT & ACTIVITIES

X-TREME
If you love speed, why not go on a jet-ski safari on double jets and race to the Red Beach and White Beach *(220 euros/2 pers.)*. Tours by speed boat for up to 12 passengers are slightly cheaper. Become airborne while parasailing *(60 euros/pers.)*. Waterski and waveboards are also offered, as well as more peaceful pedal boats *(25 euros/hr)* and double kayaks *(25 euros/hr)*. *In the centre of Períssa Beach | tel. 69 93 99 13 40 | extreme-watersports.gr*

BEACHES

PERÍSSA BEACH 👯

The fine lava sand beach starts directly below the steep Mésa Vounó hillside in the north and stretches for 5km / 3 miles along the coastline almost to Vlichóda. The beach also slopes gently into the water, making it easy to enter the sea. The centre part of the beach is also known as *Perívolos Beach* and, near Vlichóda, as *Vlichóda Beach (see p. 89)*. Sun loungers and parasols are available for hire in the Períssa and Perívolos sections, where there are also excellent water-sports facilities. *🗺 F–G 7–8*

ENTERTAINMENT

TRANQUILO BAR

A beach bar with an alternative feel. Dream the day away in hammocks in the shade of tamarisks, enjoying avocado toast and quinoa salad. In the evening, they often play live reggae. A hip venue. *Beach road, southern end | daily from 9am*

WAVES CHILL OUT

The name says it all: this is a place to chill all day long – from breakfast until the early hours. If you like massage, you can enjoy a treatment from the numerous masseuses that operate directly on the beach. *By the campsite | daily from 9am*

YAZZ

This beach bar under shady tasarisks is also open during the day. As the name suggests, jazz is the preferred music genre. *By the campsite | daily from 9am*

AROUND PERÍSSA

1 PANAGÍA TIS KATEFIÁNIS

1.5km / 1 mile from Períssa, 30 mins on foot

The white chapel high up in the rock face of Mésa Vounó is easy to spot from Períssa, but is not open to the public. To get there, follow a hiking track leading uphill to Ancient Thera. *🗺 G7*

2 ANCIENT THERA

1.7km / 1 mile from Períssa, 1 hr on foot

There is a path leading from Períssa to Ancient Thera *(see p. 69)*. It starts on the paved road from the northern end of the beach and heads inland. *🗺 G7*

3 EMBORIÓ ★

3km / 1.8 miles from Períssa, 5 mins by bus

Emborió (pop. 1,770) is one of the most interesting villages in inland Santorini. It gives you a good impression of what Santorini villages looked like in medieval times and lets you explore traditional Cycladic architecture away from the island's landmark dwellings in gorges and on the caldera edge. Two hours will be more than enough time to see this village, bearing in mind there are no tavernas or cafés.

The bus line operating between Firá and Períssa stops directly on the main village square, which also offers ample parking spaces. Eucalyptus

Sea, sand and *syrtáki*? Not really, the Yazz Beach Bar plays jazz, as its name suggests

trees provide shade on the square. Start by orienting yourself; in front of the playground next to the kiosk, turn with your back facing the street. Diagonally opposite you (approximately 300m / 1,000ft away) on the outskirts of the village, you will notice an impressively tall square tower, the *Pýrgos Goúlas (not open to the public)*. In medieval times, noble families would live in this type of fortress. They also offered the village inhabitants protection if they were plundered by pirates.

If you now gaze to your right and over the village, you will notice the village's highest landmark – and your destination if you wish to take a stroll through Emborió's narrow alleys. A blue signpost with the words "Traditional Area" in the bottom left of the square shows you which way to go. Head uphill past the village primary school (on your right) and the main church (on your left) until you reach the end of this wide path in front of a traditional mansion. Go right, and after 100m / 330ft you come to the *Ágios Spyrídonas Church* with its blue dome. Its central portal is lined by Hellenic altars with bull heads carved into the relief. The altar on your right was converted into a font at some point in the past.

Leave the churchyard and turn right down a tiny lane to the *belfries* (after approximately 20m / 65ft). Go up the lane, past the apse of the tiny church, and turn right again when you see the electricity meter with the legible number 03 350. You now enter a dark alley underneath a medieval building: one of the village's medieval *gates*. This lane leads you on to another church with a four-storey tower, the *Panagía Kalís*. You are now standing in the village's historic centre – the Kástro district – replete with narrow lanes.

Now head down the street on the south side (on the right) of the church. The alley leads you underneath another house and you will be struck by sunlight on leaving the Kástro district. You will now see an architectural feature distinctive of many medieval villages from the Venetian period on the Cyclades: there are almost no windows on the outer row of houses as it served as a city wall.

Those with an interest in art history will be treated to a gem on the road to Firá and directly opposite the village sign for Emborió: the tiny *Ágios Nikólaos Marmarítis Chapel*, whose origins as an ancient temple dating from the 3rd century BCE are still clear. The chapel measures just 3m x 4.5m (10ft x 13ft) and is without render or columns. Its walls are built from six layers of marble bricks, and the three-piece door/wall covers a tympanum *(interior not open to the public).* F7

INSIDER TIP
Recycling in antiquity

4 PERÍVOLOS
1km / 0.6 miles from Períssa, 15 mins on foot
Períssa merges almost seamlessly with the summer resort of Perívolos. Home to the island's finest and widest sandy beach, its promenade has become a trendy mile of tavernas and beach clubs packed mainly with crowds of Greek tourists from the mainland. Forget building sand castles, this beach is the place to see and be seen, where the preferred tipple is champagne rather than mineral water and deckchairs are replaced with stylish outdoor loungers. Beach volleyball is an integral part of the late afternoon programme. Those who can afford it meet up for sunset at *Seaside Santorini (tel. 22 86 08 28 01 | seasidesantorini.com | daily from 10am | €€€)*, a gourmet restaurant on the promenade, spoiling its guests with the finest fusion cuisine. The menu includes the authentic Santorini flat pea puree *fáva* with smoked eel, or a Japanese kobe steak with prawn risotto. An exquisite sushi bar is part of the establishment. Guests unwind in the evening to sounds of funky jazz, ethnic, world and, later on, Greek rock music.

5 VLICHÁDA
7km / 4 miles from Períssa, 30 mins by bicycle
Vlicháda is off the beaten track – a peaceful village that doesn't seek to show off. Central to the village is the not exactly idyllic, but very useful, harbour. In winter, almost all of Santorini's pleasure and fishing boats are safely moored here, while in summer it is the only place to offer yachts protection from the sudden Meltémi storms. The characteristic building in the village centre is a former *tomato paste factory (tomatomuseum.gr | Tue–Sun 10am–4pm | admission 10 euros)* with its tall chimney, which today is an industrial museum as well as a cultural and concert centre. In summer, the island's students display their project work at this venue, and established artists are invited to showcase their work.

After a guided tour through the old

Dramatic scenery: Vlichádá Beach is lined by steep pumice cliffs

factory buildings, where the machinery is still standing where it was once left, you can buy high-quality souvenirs in the shop and take a break in the café, enjoying local tomato juice.

Deep relaxation is provided by the ★ *Nótos Therme & Spa (by the harbour | tel. 22 86 08 11 15 | notosthermespa.com | booking required for non-hotel residents, daily 10am–7pm | chocolate bath 50 euros/45 mins).* This was a former factory which produced blocks of ice; today, it is a hotel that also offers a sauna and hammam, a thermal pool above the sea and a whirlpool in a white lava cave. Take a chocolate bath or feel the warm volcanic mud on your skin – at relatively reasonable prices.

INSIDER TIP
Melting you softly

Immediately to the south of the harbour begins *Vlichádá Beach*, which is quite light in colour and stretches for 800m / 0.5 miles in front of the low but steep shoreline to one of the best beach bars on the island: 🎦 *Théros Wave Bar*. The beach volleyball court is open to the public and the lava sand beach in front of the bar is 8–10m / 25–30ft wide and in pristine condition. The music ranges from classical and jazz to hip-hop and Greek rock (including live gigs). You get to the bar by car along a dusty track that branches off the minor tarmacked road between Vlichádá and Mégalochóri; it winds its way through a gorge with old cave dwellings and lava towers that look like art installations. Here you may

INSIDER TIP
On a desert road

be forgiven for thinking that you are in a near-eastern desert. The rough track is sprinkled with water several times a day to make sure that cars and motorbikes don't end up unrecognisable from the dust. *E8*

AKROTÍRI

(*D7*) **The name of this inland village (pop. 450) at the southwestern tip of the island is famous throughout the world because of the well-preserved archaeological remains that were excavated here in 1967, revealing one of the most spectacular and richest settlements in early European history.**

Cats know where to find shade in the centre of Akrotíri village

Around 3,600 years ago, the town was located at the sea's edge. Today, the houses, cave settlements and remains of Akrotíri are spread across the low-lying hills and lava domes between the caldera edge and wine fields. The historic centre has retained its authenticity and stretches along the main road. Akrotíri is suitable for travellers looking for a peaceful retreat with a nearby beach (15 minutes on foot) and caldera view.

SIGHTSEEING

AKROTÍRI VILLAGE
The island's oldest village is built on the slopes of a hill, on top of which stands a castle. The old centre is situated immediately to the west of the modern part of the village, along the main road with the bus stop. The *castle* itself, once the residence of a noble Venetian family until 1617, is now all but a ruin.

EATING & DRINKING

TA DELFÍNIA (THE DOLPHINS)
The most contemporary of the six tavernas at Akrotíri beach and the favourite fish restaurant among Greek tourists. There are three tables directly at the quayside and many others on the large terrace. Langoustines are left in a cage in the sea until they are ordered. *Approx. 200m / 650ft to the west of the bus terminal directly at Akrotíri Beach | tel. 22 86 08 11 51 | daily from noon | €€€*

SHOPPING

I KALÍ KARDIÁ

Michális Bélas's farming family is one of the last surviving on Santorini. His wife Ánna and their five children sell their own products from a roadside stand: delicious sun-dried tomatoes, wine, flat peas, capers and caper twigs, wild saffron, olives, sage, bay leaves, prickly pear jelly, as well as olive and tomato paste. The name of their stand translates as "good heart" – as featured on their homemade shop sign. Visitors who look as if they are genuinely interested in making a purchase will be offered free samples of all their produce. *On the main road between Akrotíri village and the lighthouse on the left, between the junctions to Kámbia and Mésa Pigádia beach*

INSIDER TIP
Genuine generosity

SPORT & ACTIVITIES

SANTO HORSERIDING 🐎

Even beginners can participate in one-hour guided hacks, and children are taken across the fields of the farm. *Near the road between the village and the excavation site | tel. 69 44 10 37 44 | santohorseriding.com | daily 8am–9pm | hack 60 euros/hr*

BEACHES

AKROTÍRI BEACH

Although this long rocky beach (350m / 1150ft) close to the excavation site is unsuitable for bathing, it has an excellent choice of fish tavernas (six in total) along the seafront. Some of them are simple and rustic, built into the lava rock caves, and belong to old locals serving authentic dishes; others have terraces perched over the water's edge with kitchens equipped with state-of-the-art appliances. ⚑ *Melina's Tavern (tel. 22 86 08 27 64 | Mon–Sat from 11.30am | melinastavernsantorini.gr | €€)* has its own art gallery built into the pumice stone cave next door, where the owner exhibits his own sculptures. Between June and September, excursion boats to the White Beach and Red Beach depart from the small quay on the beach several times a day. *1km / 0.6 miles from Akrotíri village | ⊞ D7*

ALMYRÁ BEACH 🏖

This beach (a good 150m / 490ft long) of lava pebbles, pumice stone and coarse sand has remained completely untouched by tourism; there isn't even a taverna on the seafront. A convenient place to enter the water is near the old cemented quayside at the western end of the beach. The deserted cave settlement behind the quayside was once an extremely popular fish taverna; although it operated without a licence, it was a favourite haunt of civil servants, policemen and politicians. *Along the road from Mégalochóri to Akrotíri, 1.5km / 1 mile to the west of Akrotíri (only signposted from Mégalochóri), 3.7km / 2 miles southeast of Akrotíri village | ⊞ E7–8*

CALDERA BEACH (APOTHÍKES) 🏖

The Greek name of this tiny strand situated directly below the steep caldera

A telling name: Red Beach with its light to dark red rocks

edge translates as "storerooms". Up until the mid-20th century, the inhabitants of Akrotíri had small storage huts and cave dwellings here where they kept their fishing nets and any goods they wanted to transport by ship. Today, the beach is accessed along a steep path leading down from the main road.

The path ends at the superb *Remézzo* taverna *(tel. 22 86 08 27 06 | daily from noon | €€)* which serves all kinds of fish. The terrace also has some of the island's most peculiar dried grapevines – the dead vines were originally grown in the shape of low-spiralling woven baskets. The taverna's terrace borders on the pebbly *Caldera Beach* (100m / 328ft long); the only beach on the island situated directly on the caldera. The whole bay is called *Bálos Bay. Follow the sign on the road from Mégalochóri to Akrotíri, 200m / 656ft before the junction to the lighthouse (fáros), 0.5km / 0.3 miles from Akrotíri village | ⬚ D7*

KÁMBIA BEACH

Even in August expect to find only around 40 sun loungers and 20 parasols at the pebbly Kámbia Beach. You can access the sea from the stony shore using the ladder provided, but make sure to bring bathing shoes. The cane-covered terrace belonging to *Family Snackbar Kámbia (daily | €)* accommodates just 25 guests and serves simple snacks such as *souvláki* kebabs, omelettes and salads. Only a few metres from the taverna's terrace, an impressive lava rock stack rises from the sea. From here, a coastal path takes you in 30 minutes to the Red Beach in the east, a walk on which you are unlikely to meet a soul. *2.4km / 1.6 mile south of the road from Akrotíri to Fáros, easily accessible for cars and mopeds along a signposted path, 4.3km / 2.6 miles from Akrotíri village | ⬚ D7–8*

INSIDER TIP
Remote coastline

MÉSA PIGÁDIA

Mésa Pigádia is the name of a boundary between the paved road to the lighthouse and the south coast with its rows and rows of vines. Signposted from the main road, follow a wide unpaved path (for 1.1km / 0.7 miles) to the coast where you reach a long stretch of beach (500m / 0.3 miles) in front of white pumice-stone cliffs.

Mésa Pigádia Taverna (tel. 69 84 43 26 99 | daily 11am–11.30pm | €) at the end of the path serves good food and is decorated with natural lava rock sculptures collected by the owner. The fresh fish is, for Santorini standards, affordable. Owner Valentína is a great cook and makes a first-class moussaká. *4.1km / 2.5 miles from Akrotíri village |* ⚏ *D7*

RED BEACH
(PARALÍA KÓKKINI) ★ 🌴

As maybe the island's most famous beach, it is unfortunately extremely overcrowded in summer. Covered in grey and brown coarse sand and lava pebbles, the beach (200m / 650ft long) lies in front of a steep cliff – a dramatic backdrop in various shades of red, hence the name. Many loungers under sunshades dot the beach. Getting into the water shouldn't be a problem as long as you tread carefully, and the beach has its own taverna serving simple dishes. You can reach the beach by boat from Akrotíri Beach, or by foot along the coastal path (takes 15 minutes) from the car park at the end of a road that starts at the Akrotíri excavations. *2.2km / 1.7 miles along the road from Akrotíri village, then 15 mins on foot |* ⚏ *D7–8*

WHITE BEACH
(PARALÍA ÁSPRI) 🌴 ⚑

Just 100m / 330ft long, the White Beach is only accessible by boat from Akrotíri Beach. The beach gets its name from the bright pumice-stone cliffs in the background. There are a dozen sun umbrellas dotted over the beach; you need to wade through the water to get from your boat to land. ⚏ *D7*

AROUND AKROTÍRI

🄶 EXCAVATIONS IN AKROTÍRI ★

1.5km / 0.9 miles from Akrotíri, 5 mins by car

The excavations of Europe's oldest city are well worth visiting, even for those with little interest in ancient remains. Unlike many other archaeological sites that just offer knee-high walls and traces buried in the soil, here you can see well-preserved house facades and even a small square where you would only need to place a few tables and chairs for it to resemble a typical Greek village square.

It is best to buy a few postcards or a guidebook containing Akrotíri's frescoes at the entrance so that you can get an idea of how richly this place was decorated 3,700 years ago.

> INSIDER TIP
> **Shop before you visit**

Until excavation work began here in 1974 by Spyrídon Marinátos, Crete was believed to be the main political and trading centre in the Aegean in

Railings protect the excavations from overly curious visitors

the first half of the 2nd century BCE. The Minoan palaces at Knossós, Festós, Mália and Káto Zákros, as well as estates spread over Crete, are evidence of the island's prosperity and its complex, highly organised social structure. However, only fragments of two Minoan cities were actually found on Crete: in Gourniá and Palékastro. In contrast, Akrotíri seems to have been an extremely large city with vast riches and wealth – and lies just 110km / 68 miles from the coast of Crete.

Three reasons motivated Professor Marinátos to start digging at this site. Firstly, French and German archaeologists had found pieces of pottery in the 19th century that they could not identify. Secondly, the site is also the closest point to Crete on Santorini – if there had been a city on Santorini

during the Minoan period, it would probably have been situated here. The third reason is that the pumice stone layer is thinner here than elsewhere on the island, which benefited the excavation. Incredibly, just a few hours into the excavation, the remains of the buried city were discovered; Marinátos was, however, hit by a falling wall during the excavations and died on the spot.

To view the excavations, visitors must follow a precisely marked trail which guides them along two streets on which *two- to four-storey houses* once stood; some of the facades have been preserved to their full height. Archaeologists have replaced some of the wooden segments, such as *door and window frames,* with cement (painted to resemble wood), as well as the wooden beams in the masonry to give the walls greater elasticity and earthquake protection. Some of the rooms contain *clay vessels* that have been left as they were originally found. Several houses have *stone staircases* leading to the upper floors, and *stone anchors* are also lying around. *Clay pipes* are evidence that the houses were connected to a public sewage system.

Looking at the preserved multi-story facades, you will notice that the lower rooms only had tiny windows because they were used for storage. Larger windows on the ground floor indicate that the space was used for workshops or shops. The upper rooms had windows roughly the same size as those on buildings today. At least one room in every house was painted with frescoes. Archaeologists cannot agree whether these paintings only appeared in rooms used for the practise of religious cults or also for decorating living rooms. *1.5km / 0.9 miles to the south of Akrotíri village | Apr–Oct daily 8am–8pm, Nov–Mar Tue–Sun 9am–3pm | admission 12 euros | □□ D7*

7 FÁROS (LIGHTHOUSE) ★ ☂

5km / 3 miles from Akrotíri, 10 mins by car

Towering above the southwestern-most tip of Santorini (110m / 330ft high), this lighthouse helps ships navigate into the caldera. You can reach the lighthouse by car along a well-paved road. Although the building is not open to the public, it is worth following the paths to the cape from the front of the lighthouse where you are treated to amazing views over the entire crater and to Firá, Oía and the island of Thirasía.

The last taverna before the lighthouse, *O Giorgáros (along the caldera-edge road to the lighthouse | tel. 22 86 08 30 35 | daily from 9am | €)*, is also the most southerly taverna in the Cyclades. The proprietor's family also owns three fishing boats. The speciality of the house is *rock fish*, a colourful mixture of small fish caught off Santorini's lava coast. Prices are extremely cheap for Santorini. □□ C7

Akrotíri
Excavations

A Odós Telkhiron
B Triangular Square
C North Mill
D Tunnel

Alpha Block
D
North Stores
A
House of Women
West House
b
Delta Block
Xeste 2
Gamma Sector
A
Beta Block
Xeste 3
Xeste 4

FRESCOES
a Women, Papyrus
b Youth with bundles of fish, Animal hunt in river
c Lilies
d Monkeys
e Antelope Children boxing
f Maidens

30m
33 yds

OÍA & THE NORTH

A BEAUTY FULL OF GALLERIES

What's the difference? Similar to Firá, many houses in Oía are situated directly on the caldera edge, stretching far down the steep hillsides. However, Oía doesn't just face the caldera but also the open Aegean sea, and the neighbouring islands of Íos and Síkinos form part of the town's backdrop.

Here, the caldera-edge promenade resembles a long shopping mall – packed mainly with art galleries where you can effortlessly spend a small fortune. On Ammoúdi pier, one of the two tiny

A sight to behold: Oía clings organically to the lava cliffs

harbours of this small town, you can eat some of the best fish in the world while seated between lava cliffs and the ocean waves. But, above all, Oía is renowned for its incredible sunsets. This is why, from late afternoon onwards, endless crowds of people wander the narrow lanes to the ruins of Lóndsa Fort – the best place to watch the sun set on the sea horizon. Therefore, it is better to visit Oía (pronounced "ee-ah" not "oy-ah") in late morning, in this way avoiding the masses of cruise-ship tourists.

OÍA & THE NORTH

Katharós Beach

Maritime Museum **2**

4 Ammoúdi ★

 Katína

3
Lónds Fort ★

MARCO POLO HIGHLIGHTS

★ **LÓNDSA FORT**
Where the Aegean Sea becomes a stage
➤ p. 100

★ **AMMOÚDI**
A harbour like no other ➤ p. 100

★ **BAXÉDES BEACH**
A long and peaceful beach ➤ p. 105

Baxédes Beach ★

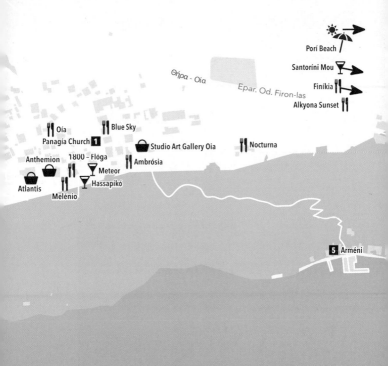

Porí Beach

Santoríni Mou

Θήρα - Οία

Epar. Od. Firon-Ias

Finíkia

Alkyona Sunset

Oía

Blue Sky

Panagía Church **1**

Studio Art Gallery Oia

Nocturna

Anthemion

1800 – Flóga

Ambrósia

Meteor

Atlantis

Hassapikó

Melénio

5 Arméni

100 m
109 yd

OÍA

(📖 C-D2) **By amalgamating with the once-independent neighbouring settlements of Finíkia and Perívolos, Oía (pop. 1,000) has witnessed a similar urban development to Firá along the caldera, and now slopes down the island's western hillside until it reaches Thólos.**

The majority of hotels and apartment complexes are built on the caldera side, along the promenade lined with lots of shops, cafés and tavernas.

Although Oía is not a beach resort, if you're a keen beach-goer it serves as a good base if you are prepared to walk half an hour along the footpath to the nearest beaches; otherwise hire a vehicle for the duration of your stay.

SIGHTSEEING

🖬 PANAGÍA CHURCH

The town's main church is situated on a tiny square nestled between the caldera-edge promenade and the central bus terminal. You are bound to pass it at some point during your visit, so why not have a look inside. You will certainly find some respite there from the crowds of tourists in the lanes. The interior is decorated with several new frescoes in traditional Byzantine style. You may be able to find depictions of the birth of Jesus or the crucifixion. *Usually freely accessible in the morning and late afternoon | ⏱ 5–10 mins*

🖬 MARITIME MUSEUM

Housed in a pretty classicist-style villa and organised over two floors, this small museum exhibits nautical equipment, model ships of former Santorini ship owners and a row of historical photos showing Oía prior to the 1956 earthquake, at a time when it had not become dependent on tourism. The showpiece among the museum's artefacts is the 250-year old wooden galleon figure taken from a sailing boat built in Oía: it depicts an attractive lady with an ample cleavage revealing one of her breasts. *On the caldera-edge promenade (signposted) | Apr–mid-Nov Wed–Mon 10am–2pm and 5–7pm| admission 4 euros | ⏱ 20 mins*

🖬 LÓNDSA FORT ★

One of Santorini's most spectacular panoramas is from this ruined castle at the pinnacle point of Oía. You not only have far-reaching views over the caldera and village, but also to the neighbouring islands of Íos and Folégandros, and, on clear days, even to Síkinos. In medieval times, the fort was the seat of the noble Venetian Argýri family. Most of the fort had already been destroyed by the 19th century; it has now been restored as a viewing platform and welcomes crowds of visitors for the island's sunset. *Open to the public*

🖬 AMMOÚDI ★ 🚩

It is likely that you haven't seen a "harbour" quite like this before. The narrow pier is perched below the caldera's lava walls and offers just

Ammoúdi: freshly caught octopus will soon be on your plate

enough space for a handful of tavernas. Apart from a few tiny boats, the small ferry to the neighbouring island of Thirasía docks here several times a day. The harbour is reached on foot from Lóndsa Fort via a great number of steps. You can get there by car as well, but it is almost impossible to find a parking space.

A 250-m / 820-ft long path leads south from the tavernas to the *Cape of Ágios Nikólaos,* off which lies the *Ágios Nikólaos* islet with its tiny chapel. Those with a sense of adventure can climb down the steps into the sea and swim the small distance

INSIDER TIP
Brave the waves

(15m / 50ft) to the islet (bathing shoes are advisable).

5 ARMÉNI

Up until the earthquake in 1956, the tiny port of Arméni was still producing wooden fishing boats, so-called *kaikis,* and yachts, as can be seen in photos on display in the Maritime Museum in Oía. Excursion boats for trips around the caldera now depart from here. Small boat repairs are done on a single wharf. On the hot haul back up to Oía, a tiny *taverna* offers refreshment and food. The port can be reached by steep stairs, which start in the centre of the caldera-edge promenade. It takes around 15–20 minutes to get down.

EATING & DRINKING

1800 FLÓGA

This fine restaurant serves up creative Greek cuisine in a restored cave dwelling – a feast for the eyes! Indoors you will find a classic and elegant ambience, whereas the roof terrace has caldera views. Booking is recommended. *Caldera-edge promenade, by the turning to Arméni harbour | tel. 22 86 07 14 85 | oia-1800.com | daily from noon | €€€*

ALKYONA SUNSET

Although this modest taverna lies on the main thoroughfare, it is worth visiting for its homemade dishes passed on through generations of this family-run business. You can watch the cook fill and roll up her vine leaves in the morning. There is, however, one break from tradition: these days you can also get vegetarian moussaká. *Just before the main car park | tel. 22 86 07 12 42 | daily from noon | €*

AMBRÓSIA

This high-end restaurant with marvellous views serves fabulous Mediterranean cuisine. The chef's creativity is unrivalled and rather spellbinding. How about grilled octopus in *kataífi* pastry with *taramá* and mint sauce as an hors d'oeuvre? Then try duck in vinsanto sauce as the main course. For pudding, you could have *kataífi* with mastic ice cream and pink pepper! It is recommended that you reserve a table and bring either a full wallet or your credit card. *Central location bn the Aegean side of the caldera-edge promenade | tel. 22 86 07 14 13, restaurant-ambrosia.com | daily 6.30–10.30pm | €€€*

BLUE SKY

Along the short walk from the bus stop to the caldera-edge promenade, this restaurant with its large shady terrace, but without sea or caldera views, serves typical taverna food at acceptable prices. We recommend the lamb

ONE MINUTE IS ALL IT TOOK

In 1956, Santorini was struggling with enough problems already: the Greek civil war, which lasted from the end of World War II to 1949, had only ended seven years before. After years of hunger during both wars, the island had been left in poverty. On 9 July 1956 at 5.30am, the citizens were awoken by the ground shaking. An earthquake with a magnitude of 7.8 was measured on the Richter scale, and it demolished 40 per cent of all the island's houses in a matter of one minute, leaving 50 people dead. Oía and Firá on the caldera edge were the worst affected villages. Over 250 aftershocks were registered over the next 24 hours, which caused parts of the crater rock to fall, crashing into the sea. Thousands of inhabitants deserted the island and many never returned. Only the expansion of tourism at the beginning of the 1970s helped Santorini finally recover from this shock.

shank. *Tel. 22 86 07 11 79 | daily 9am–10pm | €–€€*

FINÍKIA

A wood-fired oven is the centrepiece of this taverna. It's used to bake bread and other specialities, including stuffed lamb with potatoes, filo pastry filled with meat, and baklavás. Mussels cooked in white wine and turkey with figs are also worth trying. *Finíkia, on the main road | tel. 22 86 07 13 73 | daily from 8.30am | €€-€€€*

KATÍNA

One of three fish tavernas at Santorini's most picturesque port. The owner, Katína, is a friendly old lady who runs the restaurant with her three sons. Fish and seafood are standard on the menu and are served with a very good wine from the island. *Ammoúdi | tel. 22 86 07 12 80 | fishtavernkatina.gr | Mon–Sat noon–10.30pm, Sun noon–9pm | €€*

Katína taverna in Ammoúdi

MELÉNIO

Santorini's best-known pâtisserie, with an amazing selection of traditional European cakes and oriental pastries such as baklavás and *kataífi*. *On the Aegean side of the caldera-edge promenade | May–Oct daily, open all hours*

NOCTURNA 🐷

Of all restaurants directly by the caldera edge, this simple one located above a supermarket offers best value for money. The food is okay, and no more, but the view across Oía and the caldera is just as beautiful as elsewhere. Pizza, pasta, ice cream and cocktails are on the menu. *In the southern part of the caldera-edge promenade | tel. 22 86 07 12 20 | daily from 9.30am | €–€€*

OÍA 🐷

You wouldn't have thought it possible, but you can eat well in Oía even on a small budget. This barbecue taverna, with its small terrace, serves gyros – not only as a full dish, but also in pítta bread *(3 euros)* and on small skewers. *10m / 30ft from the bus stop | €*

SHOPPING

ANTHEMION

Vassilikí Savváni insists that her outlet is not a "shop", but the "headquarters of fantasy". Every last detail of her puppets, which are up to a metre tall, is designed by herself. Vassilikí gets the ideas for her creations from fairy tales, legends and dreams. *Caldera-edge promenade | anthemion.com.gr*

ATLANTIS

You need to see this international bookshop. A few steps lead down into the house built straight into the caldera's wall. Despite the small space and apparent chaos, everything is actually in perfect order. The shop has a large variety of older books about the island

be great to prepare you for your next holiday in the country. *Caldera-edge promenade | atlantisbooks.org*

STUDIO ART GALLERY OÍA

Watercolours painted by the Greek artist Sivridákis, who you will probably meet in the gallery. He specialises in Santorini landscapes, which are also sold as affordable prints or postcards. *Caldera-edge promenade between the town centre and Lóndsa Fort*

INSIDER TIP
Affordable art

Atlantis bookshop: browse a good selection of books in the caldera

INSIDER TIP
Alphabet wall hanging

in many languages. Here, you can also buy a poster with the small and capital letters of the Greek alphabet, which will

SPORT & ACTIVITIES

HIKING TO MÉSA VOUNÓ

There is a relaxing alternative to the sunset view from Lóndsa Fort: a half-hour hike hike from the southern edge of the village will take you to the *Profítis Ilías Chapel* just below the peak of 331m / 1,080ft high Mésa Vounó. It is best to start from Hotel Atlantída Villas in the Finíkia part of town. Since there is no lighting along the track, we recommend that you bring a torch for the return.

BEACHES

BAXÉDES BEACH ★ ⁂

This wide open beach with coarse sand and lava pebbles stretches for 3km / 1.8 miles along the Aegean Sea with white pumice-stone cliffs in the background. It goes from the northern tip of Mavrópetra to the tip of Koloúmbos in the south. The coastline is largely undeveloped and offers far-reaching views of the Aegean. A handful of tavernas and a few B&Bs can be found along the steep cliff or on the inland side of the promenade. The centre of the beach is referred to as *Parádissos Beach,* and the east part as *Koloúmbos Beach*. There are no parasols or sun loungers for hire and no water-sports facilities. A bus service runs several times a day between Oía and the beach during the main season. *3.5–7km / 2–4.5 miles from the bus terminal in Oía | ▥ D1*

KATHARÓS BEACH ⁂

Along the road between Oía and Ammoúdi, a 200-m / 650-ft long path branches off to your right. At the end, go down a short footpath to reach the narrow stretch of beach (80m / 260ft long) with dark lava sand. The beach is

virtually deserted outside the main season. There are no sun loungers or parasols to hire, but the surrounding cliffs provide a little shade. The *Kátharos Lounge* beach bar, located directly above the beach, is open in high summer, and its canvas-covered terrace nestles between impressive lava and pumice-rock formations. ▥ C1–2

PORÍ BEACH ⁂

Set in front of a steep low coastline, this long dark lava-pebble beach (1.4km / 0.8 miles) is nearly always empty, except in July and August – almost unheard of on Santorini! There are no sun umbrellas or sun loungers for hire, and there is no bus service. *6.5km / 4 miles from Oía | ▥ E1–2*

WELLNESS

SANTORINI PREMIUM SPA

This public hotel spa offers treatments and rejuvenating baths in a small and intimate wellness area. You can swim in the hotel pool in the courtyard, and in between or afterwards enjoy their excellent cuisine. Of course, this kind of luxury comes at a price: a one-hour, four-hand massage for a couple, including lunch by the pool, costs 200 euros. You will pay the same for a feel-good package for one person, including Cleopatra Bath, four-hand massage and spa lunch. *Museum Hotel, caldera-edge promenade | tel. 22 86 07 15 08 | short.travel/san6*

SUNSET MASSAGE

Experience the sunset off Oía in an individual and totally different way:

First, relax with a glass of wine on the private terrace, and then enjoy a couples massage in romantically designed lava caves in the caldera wall *(298 euro/couple | ⏱ 2½ hours). Near the fort | tel. 22 86 88 80 08 | sunset-massages.com*

NIGHTLIFE

HASSAPIKÓ
After those who have come to see the sunset have gone home, this rather small and inconspicuous bar in the central section of the caldera-edge promenade next to the characteristic belfry is the hotspot in town all year round. Owner Marykay knows many of her patrons by name, and Morocco-born DJ Christoph Kardek is a producer with his own label. *hassapiko. gr | daily from 8am*

METEOR
There is no view of the caldera at sunset from here, but the terrace of this small bar is the perfect place to indulge in a spot of people-watching as there are many passers-by. Enjoy your sundowner at this "fashion show". The

INSIDER TIP
Shop for antiques
antiques used to decorate the terrace and interior of this classicist-style building are available to buy. *Caldera-edge promenade, on the way to Lóndsa Fort | daily*

SANTORÍNI MOU
The taverna's name translates as "My Santoríni". Located on the main road in the district of Finíkia (which means "palms", by the way), its idyllic,

flower-filled garden terrace is a delightful setting to enjoy the taverna's home-style Greek food. Live Greek music is often played from 10pm. *Tel. 22 86 07 13 30 | daily from 6.30pm | €€*

AROUND OÍA

THIRASÍA
2.5km / 1.5 miles from Ammoúdi harbour to Ríva, 15 mins by passenger ferry
Are you longing for a desert island? Passenger ferries depart from Ammoúdi harbour in Oía several times a day to the port of Ríva on Santoríni's smaller neighbour, Thirasía. From there it is 3km / 1.8 miles to the island's main resort, Manólas with a population of just 160. There are often taxis and a bus waiting at the port to collect tourists. It is worth visiting Manólas for its tranquillity and the stunning view of Santoríni. *Contact the harbour police in Firá for information on the ferry connections: 100m / 330ft to the left of the platía, direction Oía | tel. 22 86 02 22 39 | ⎅ A–C 2–4*

SIGÁLAS WINE FACTORY
1.5km / 1 mile from Oía, 5 mins by car
Páris Sigálas was a mathematics teacher before he turned his attention to organic viticulture in 1991. Since then, he has built his own 7-hectare organic vineyard and also pays winegrowers premiums if they turn their fields over to organic farming. His winery produces approximately 75,000

A new vintage, soon to be tested at Sigálas winery

bottles a year. Excursion buses are a seldom sight at this winery, so you can taste the wines at your leisure on the vine-covered terrace while enjoying the view over the Aegean. *1.5km / 1 mile below the road between Oía–Firá (signs from the main road in Finíkia), 3km / 1.8 miles from the bus terminal square in Oía | sigalas-wine.com | Apr, Oct, Nov Mon–Fri 10am–7pm, Sat/Sun 11am–7pm, May, Sept Mon–Fri 10am–8pm, Sat/Sun 11am –8pm, Jun–Aug Mon–Fri 10am –9.30pm, Sat/Sun 11am–9.30pm | ⏠ D2*

PORÍ
8km / 5 miles from Oía, 15 mins by car
The tiny port of Porí lies to the south of Porí Beach and resembles a port on the Azores archipelago island of Pico due to its setting surrounded by dark lava cliffs. It is one of the least fre quented beaches on the island. | ⏠ E2

ÁGIOS ARTÉMIOS
9km / 5.5 miles from Oía, 15 mins by car
This solitary church lies slightly ele- vated above the island's eastern coastline. In its vicinity are several pil- grim retreats, some built inside the flower-filled cemetery and some opposite the church carved from the lava rock walls. The retreats are only used once a year for the main patron saint festival on 19 and 20 October. *Sat/Sun 10am–1pm | ⏠ F2*

DISCOVERY TOURS

If you are keen to discover the sights of the island, these discovery tours provide a perfect guide.

① SANTORINI AT A GLANCE

- ➤ Enjoy the view towards Crete from the lighthouse
- ➤ Take a boat trip to the Red Beach
- ➤ Stop for a swim at Kamári

📍	Firá	🏁	Firá
🔄	105km / 65 miles	🚗	2 days (3½ hrs total driving time)

DAY 1	**CONNECTIONS BETWEEN SANTORINI AND CRETE**
① Firá	Pick up your rental car at 9.30am in ① Firá ➤ p. 42 *and follow the road along the caldera edge to the* ② Lighthouse ➤ p. 95 at the tip of the cape of Akrotíri. You'll have amazing views over the wide-open sea to Crete on one side and of the entire caldera on the other. Head
14km 15 mins	
② Lighthouse	

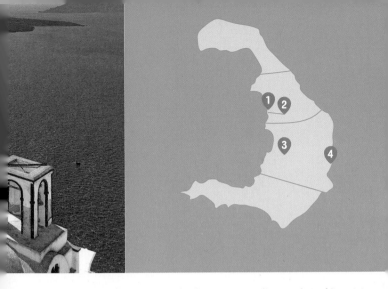

Firá first: the island's capital is the starting point for a round trip of Santorini

back to the village of Akrotíri and *drive to its other side* where you can spend an hour visiting the ❸ excavations ➤ p. 93 of Ancient Akrotíri. Then *wander down to the quay from where you can hire a small boat* to spend an hour bathing and relaxing at ❹ Red Beach ➤ p. 93.

SWIMMING, SUNBATHING & SPORT

Return to the quay by around 2pm for lunch at the fish taverna ❺ Ta Delfínia ➤ p. 90 on Akrotíri's waterfront. After a leisurely meal, *drive back along the caldera-edge road and after a short while take the turn-off to Vlicháda ➤ p. 88*. There, you can visit the former ❻ tomato-paste factory, with its unmissable chimney. After that, enjoy a long, relaxing break at ❼ Períssa Beach ➤ p. 86 with a refreshing drink at Beachclub Chilli, before trying your hand at water paragliding, which is offered just next door by Wave Sports ➤ p. 35; you can enjoy a bird's-eye view of Santorini while being towed through the air by a boat *(80 euros /2 pers.)*!

SHOPPING BY THE ROADSIDE

After a coffee at Yazz ➤ p. 86 (level with Vlicháda's campsite), set off on your route again by 6pm. *Head back to the caldera-edge road again and, right at the*

6.5km	15 mins
❸ **Excavations**	
1.5km	25 mins
❹ **Red Beach**	
1km	15 mins
❺ **Ta Delfínia**	
8km	20 mins
❻ **Tomato paste factory**	
5.5km	5 mins
❼ **Períssa Beach**	
9km	10 mins

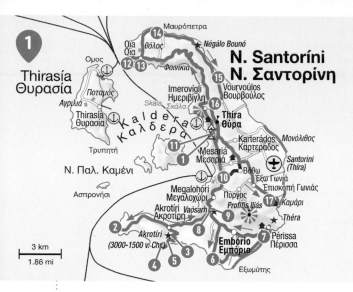

N. Santoríni
N. Σαντορίνη

8 Galatéa's Pottery Studio

100m 2 mins

9 Art Centre Akrón

3.5km 5 mins

junction where you reach it, stop for an exclusive shopping break: **8** Galatéa's Pottery Studio ➤ p. 79 sells pretty ceramics, while ancient art replicas are available at **9** Art Centre Akrón ➤ p. 79.

A GLASS OF WINE AT SUNSET

After shopping, *you'll pass the access road to the Athínios Port and on your left* you will soon notice the large, modern **10** Sántos Winery ➤ p. 76, right on the caldera edge. Enjoy the sunset here with a glass of Santorini wine *before returning to* **11** Firá. Good and relatively cheap accommodation is available at Hotel Summertime *(summertime-santorini.com)*, situated along the road signposted to the campsite. Just a 10 minute walk from the hotel is the Náoussa taverna ➤ p. 51, an ideal spot for dinner.

10 Sántos Winery

4.5km 5 mins

11 Firá

EXPLORING OÍA

DAY 2

14km 20 mins

12 Ammoúdi

1.5km 5 mins

The second day starts at 9.30am, again in Firá. This time, *take the road along the caldera edge, heading north. You pass through the island's most northerly town, Oía, and follow the road down to* **12** Ammoúdi ➤ p. 100, with especially spectacular views into the caldera. Then *drive back up to* ⑬ Oía ➤ p. 100 where a parking space will be easy to find at this time of day. *Proceed on foot to the caldera-edge promenade and follow it to the* Lóndsa Fort ➤ p. 100. On your walk back to the car, take a quick peek in the Maritime Museum ➤ p. 100, followed by a stop at pâtisserie Melénio ➤ p. 103, with another splendid view over the caldera.

THE QUIET NORTHEAST

Set off in your car around 1.30pm to Tholos and *down to the island's north coast.* ⑭ Delfíni taverna (daily | €), above the small fishing shelter port at Cape Mavrópetra, is a good spot for a salad or fish soup for lunch. *Your journey then continues past several tiny beaches to the* ⑮ Ágios Artémios Church ➤ p. 107, which is worth a quick visit. After that, the road now heads off inland and uphill. You reach the village of *Vourvoúlos* ➤ *p. 56; drive through it and turn right below the tiny, traditional Santorini cemetery.* Take the opportunity to take a look in one or two of the numerous, desolate ⑯ cave dwellings which you pass.

STROLLING & BATHING

Take the main road between Oía and Firá, turn left and when you arrive in Firá follow the sign to ⑰ Kamári ➤ p. 62. You should arrive here by around 4pm. Park your car at the end of the main road on the large seafront car park. This is where the town's long seaside promenade begins. Follow it to the water-sports centre, located in the centre of the main beach, Kamári Beach ➤ p. 66. Enjoy a dip in the sea, followed by an evening meal at the authentic Salíveros Tavern ➤ p. 64 directly on the promenade. Walk northwards into the resort to end your day at the Club Albatross ➤ p. 66 on the seafront, listening to international music and dancing *syrtáki*.

It's less than a 15-minute drive back to ❶ Firá ➤ p. 42. Enjoy a glass of sangria made from Santorini wine as a nightcap at Kirá Thirá ➤ p. 56.

⑬ Oía
4.5km   25 mins

⑭ Delfíni taverna
6.5km   10 mins

⑮ Ágios Artémios Church
2km   5 mins

⑯ Cave dwellings
10.5km   15 mins

⑰ Kamári
10km   20 mins

❶ Firá

② CALDERA-EDGE WALK FROM FIRÁ TO OÍA

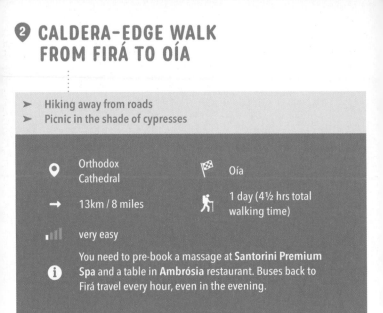

➤ Hiking away from roads
➤ Picnic in the shade of cypresses

◉ Orthodox Cathedral

🏁 Oía

→ 13km / 8 miles

🥾 1 day (4½ hrs total walking time)

▮▮▮ very easy

ⓘ You need to pre-book a massage at **Santorini Premium Spa** and a table in **Ambrósia** restaurant. Buses back to Firá travel every hour, even in the evening.

① Orthodox Cathedral
2.5km 45 mins
② Ágios Nikólaos
50m 1 min
③ Imerovígli
700m 15 mins
④ Skáros rock
900m 30 mins
⑤ Mini-market

THE OVERTURE

From the ① Orthodox Cathedral ➤ p. 44 in Firá *follow the caldera-edge promenade northwards*. Passing the *Archaeological Museum* ➤ p. 44 and the cable-car station, and through Firostefáni, you reach ② Ágios Nikólaos ➤ p. 48, a tiny convent. A few steps further and you arrive in ③ Imerovígli. The next section *takes you away from the caldera edge at the Blue Note restaurant, and climbs 100m / 328ft down a narrow path in the caldera wall* to the ④ Skáros rock ➤ p. 49 where there are the remains of a small castle. Those who want to get a closer look at the castle should be surefooted. *Climb back up to the caldera-edge promenade. Take the stairs right behind the Blue Note Restaurant*, which go past the Rocka Cafebar to the small *platia* in Imerovigli. *There, you turn left after the Hotel La Maltese, then left again, and take the first lane on the right* passing by the apartment complex "Vallais Villas". You will reach a short section of paved road with a small, nameless ⑤ mini-market, where you can buy everything you need for a picnic and water, of course. *The route ahead is now clearly discernible again.*

PICNIC

Take a short break at the ❻ Iris taverna *(daily | €€)* right on the caldera edge for a coffee or tea and maybe some tzatziki with bread, because this could be your last chance to grab a bite to eat before Oía. A few minutes later you pass a small group of hotels and a traditional Santorini cemetery. *The path starts to climb once you pass the Santorini My Spa hotel complex. The road forks into*

Skáros rock

two directions in front of the To Monopáti café; *keep right to reach* ❼ Ágios Márkos, *where you can unpack your picnic on the church's round stone bench in the shade of the cypress trees.*

❹ Iris taverna	
2km	35 mins

❼ Ágios Márkos	
300m	5 mins

THE MOST CHALLENGING LEG

Your route now continues along a narrow concrete road up to the ❽ Profítis Ilías chapel ➤ p. 71 on the hill with the same name. The road now becomes a path where you tread along lava and pumice rock chippings. After around 15 minutes on this slippery path, the route becomes sturdier underfoot again, *joining the road from Firá to Oía, which now crosses the narrowest point on the island with simultaneous views across the caldera and out to sea.*

❽ Profítis Ilías chapel	
2km	35 mins

After just a few minutes you reach a simple open-air refreshment ❾ bar selling a delicious home-made walnut cake baked fresh by the owner almost every day. *Next to the bar is the start of a red and white path marked "hiking route 1",* which takes you in 30–40 minutes to the ❿ Tímios Stavrós chapel at an altitude of 270m / 886ft.

❾ bar	
1.5km	30-40 mins

❿ Tímios Stavrós chapel	
2.5km	40 mins

THE FINAL STRETCH

You can now see Oía in front of you. The path leads *downwards across a lava field to the village's first houses, where it joins the main road. You then come to a small*

⑪ Oía

square which connects to the caldera-edge promenade in ⑪ Oía ➤ p. 100. *Stroll along the promenade through the entire village.* It is now around 2pm and time for a light lunch. To your left, located on the roof above a supermarket, Café Nocturna *(daily | €€)* serves basic, affordable food without having to pay extra for the caldera view.

SUNSET IN OÍA

After a bite to eat, shopping is on the agenda. Have a look into the many small galleries along the caldera-edge promenade. It's now around 5pm and time to relax (provided you have pre-booked a massage): enjoy an hour of pampering at Santorini Premium Spa ➤ p. 105. Afterwards continue to the

Lóndsa Fort ➤ p. 100, where you won't be the only one waiting for the perfect sunset. Join the crowds and have your camera ready for a great picture! Now *head back a few paces on the caldera-edge promenade* and dine in the Ambrósia restaurant ➤ p. 102. From there, it is just five minutes to the bus terminal *(single ticket 2 euros)*.

❸ THE OTHER FACE OF SANTORINI: A WALK WITH AEGEAN VIEWS

➤ **Climb Santorini's highest peak**
➤ **Explore a windswept ancient city**

📍 Pýrgos	🏁 God's Garden taverna
→ 13km / 8 miles	🥾 1 day (4½–5 hrs total walking time)
📶 easy	

A PICTURESQUE VILLAGE

This tour starts at the village square in ❶ Pýrgos ➤ p. 75, which is also a stop on the bus route. Steps lead up from the square through the maze of alleys in the old centre to the Kástro district and a ❷ bastion, where, for the first time, you have wide views over other parts of the island. Back on the village square after your warm-up, head to the ❸ supermarket to pick up water and food for a picnic during your ascent of Profítis Ilías.

REACHING THE TOP

The route now climbs gently along the main road. After 700m / 2,300ft, you will see a wooden signpost which is soon replaced by a red and white waymark numbered 1. Approximately 200m / 656ft before the Profítis Ilías chapel, the path joins the paved road again. In front of the gate to the antenna station on the 567-m / 1,860-ft high summit of ❹ Profítis Ilías ➤ p. 71, *the entrance to the path down to Ancient Thera is signposted.* At

❶ Pýrgos	
200m	5 mins
❷ bastion	
300m	6 mins
❸ supermarket	
3km	1½ hrs
❹ Profítis Ilías	
1.5km	40 mins

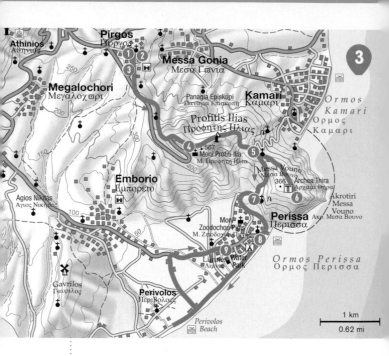

times, the path will take you over narrow ridges and through thorny sections and herbs; it goes *right down to the Selláda mountain pass* between the peaks of Profítis Ilías and Mésa Vounó. It is worth taking your picnic break halfway down this section to soak up the captivating panorama.

AN ANCIENT CITY ABOVE THE SEA

A **5** drinks stand is usually open at the Selláda mountain pass car park, selling coffee and small snacks. *Follow the paved path past a block of toilets to the entrance to* **6** Ancient Thera ➤ p. 69. The excavation site is situated in pristine landscape on a narrow rocky plateau jutting far out into the Aegean; its ancient walls perfectly complement the wild landscape around. Spend one and a half hours exploring the site before continuing on your route. *Follow the signpost from the car park kiosk down to Périssa*. On the way it is worth taking a short detour to the **7** Panagía tis Katefiánis chapel ➤ p. 86 high above the coastal resort.

5 drinks stand

| 800m | 30 mins |

6 Ancient Thera

| 2km | 50 mins |

7 Panagía tis Katefiánis chapel

| 700m | 10 mins |

A HIP HANGOUT: PÉRISSA

In *Teríssa* ➤ *p. 84*, first go straight to the resort's beautiful sandy ❽ Teríssa Beach ➤ p. 86 for a leisurely swim to relax your weary legs. Then hire a pedal boat for an hour on the water at Wave Sports ➤ p. 35, before enjoying an early evening meal around 6pm at the ❾ God's Garden taverna ➤ p. 85: *also situated on the main road further on in the direction of Mésa Vounó*. The taverna serves authentic Santorini specialities at relatively cheap prices. The bus stop is just a few metres from the restaurant.

❽ **Teríssa Beach**
4.5km   1 hr

❾ **God's Garden taverna**

❹ AROUND SANTORINI'S AIRPORT BY MOPED

➤ Explore a hidden village
➤ Visit Santorini's oldest church

📍 Kamári	🏁 Cíne Kamári
↻ 19km / 12 miles	🚲 1 day (1½–2 hrs total driving time)

The tour kicks off with a leisurely start in ❶ Kamári ➤ p. 62 where you take *the road in the direction of Firá*. Take a brief glance at the evening's film programme at Cíne Kamári ➤ p. 66 (on the outskirts of Kamári) before following the sign leading left to the ancient church ❷ Panagía Episkopí ➤ p. 71 with its pretty gardens. *Back on the main road, ride for around 300m/ 984ft before following the next sign pointing left* to the cave gallery ❸ Art Space ➤ p. 72, a contemporary art-house set in an old wine cellar carved from pumice stone where you can also try the wine that is stored there.

AFTER THE BREAK, A CHURCH VISIT

Back on the main road continue for 3km / 2 miles to dine on large portions of pork chops and delicious salads at the ❹ Kritikós taverna ➤ p. 74. *A narrow road opposite the taverna winds along one of Santorini's typical*

❶ **Kamári**
2km   15 mins

❷ **Panagía Episkopí**
1.5km   10 mins

❸ **Art Space**
3km   15 mins

❹ **Kritikós taverna**
500m   5 mins

inland gorges, lined with agaves and cave dwellings in the pumice stone walls. Take a break in the completely tranquil village of ❺ Vóthonas ➤ p. 74. **INSIDER TIP** With luck, someone will pass by and **A key moment** you can ask them for the key to the ❻ Panagía tis Sergína chapel. Key in hand, leave your moped at the end of the road and walk for five minutes along the tiny path further up into the gorge to see the inside of this unique cave church. Then head back to the main road and continue for 400m / 1,310ft to the island's photogenic ❼ Wine Museum ➤ p. 73.

BEACHES, A FABULOUS TAVERNA & A SUMMER CINEMA

By the time you're ready to go, it is probably already 4.30pm and time to *follow the signs to the airport. Drive around the northern end of the runway to* ❽ Monólithos ➤ p. 67 with its excellent *beach ➤ p. 66.* and bathing opportunities – don't hesitate to go for a

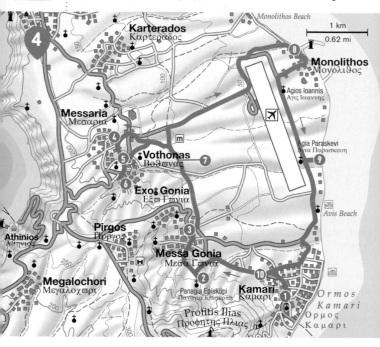

Pretty details: Panagía Episkopí in Kamári is one of the oldest churches on Santorini

swim! *After a splash in the sea, drive along the coastal road parallel to the airport runway in the direction of Kamári. A small sign points the way to* Agía Paraskeví Beach *and the solitary* ❾ Galíni taverna ➤ p.63 which, for your dinner, serves the small locally caught fish, a speciality rarely found in the island's tavernas. *Just 3km/2 miles further in Kamári*, you can enjoy a special treat: a wonderful open-air cinema under the island's starry skies at the ❿ Cíne Kamári ➤ p. 66.

❾ **Galíni taverna**

3km 15 mins

❿ **Cíne Kamári**

GOOD TO KNOW

HOLIDAY BASICS

ARRIVAL

GETTING THERE

There are many chartered flights to Santorini from the UK during the summer months. EasyJet and British Airways also offer direct seasonal flights from Manchester and London. The average flight time from London to Santorini is four hours. A stop over in Athens will be your only way of reaching the island outside the main season. Santorini airport lies between Kamári and Monólithos. A taxi to Firá is approx. 15 euros. An airport shuttle bus service runs during the summer season between 5.30am and 10.25pm; the fare to Firá is approx. 2 euros. Hire cars are available at the airport.

+ 2 hours ahead

Greece is two hours ahead of Greenwich Mean Time, seven hours ahead of US Eastern Time and seven hours behind Australian Eastern Time.

Adapter Type C

You will need a European adapter type C.

There are several car ferries a day running between Piraeus and Santorini. They can take between 7½

This is where the shuttle boats for the cruise liners dock: the old port of Fíra

and 11½ hours depending on how many stops on other islands they make. Catamarans also transport vehicles and take just 4–5 hours but are twice as expensive. *For timetables see gtp.gr.*

Regular public buses run between the main port of Athínios and Firá.

Another alternative is to fly to Iráklio on Crete, visit the Minoan treasures at the Archaeological Museum and Knossós, and then cross to Santorini by car ferry or catamaran the next day. *Timetables are available at gtp.gr, seajets.gr, minoan.gr.*

INSIDER TIP
Land on Crete

GETTING IN

A valid passport is required for entry into Greece. Children need their own passport.

CLIMATE & WHEN TO GO

The high season on Santorini is April to October. Many hotels and restaurants are closed in the other months. In May, the sea can still be too cold for swimming, but this is the month when flowers are in bloom all over the island. Temperatures often reach above 30°C / 86°F by day and do not drop below 20°C / 68 °F at night during July and August. The water is pleasantly warm in autumn, but the vegetation is largely withered and burnt.

It hardly rains between June and August, but pack a rain jacket for the occasional rainstorm. There are often very strong – and pleasant – winds in high summer, so always carry a jacket or pullover with you. The sun is often strong, so don't forget to apply sun lotion!

GETTING AROUND

BUS

Buses serve routes from Firá to all towns and villages, the airport and the main port of Athínios. Up-to-date timetables are on display at the bus terminal in Firá or online (with ticket prices) at *ktel-santorini.gr*. There are also shuttle services to the beaches at Vlichádi and Perívolos during high season. Tickets are purchased on the bus from the conductor. Prices are cheap: 1.80 euros from Firá to Kamári, 2.30 euros from Firá to Veríssa and from Firá to Akrotíri. Note that you have to buy a new ticket every time you change buses.

VEHICLE HIRE

Bicycles, mopeds, trikes, quad bikes, motor scooters and cars can be rented in all of the holiday resorts. Prices vary depending on the season, ranging from 150 euros a week in May to 350 euros per week in August for the same type of car.

To rent a car or moped, you will need your driver's licence and be at least 21 or 18 years old respectively.

Even if you have full insurance cover, damage to the tyres and the underside of the car is often not covered. Make sure you read the rental terms and conditions beforehand. No matter how minor the accident, you should call the hire company – otherwise, the insurance company will not pay.

TAXI

There are only about 40 taxis on the island. You can flag taxis down on the street, get in at a taxi rank or call for one. There are taxi ranks in Firá and at the airport. The prices are set by the government and are comparatively low. Taxi drivers are generally honest, but you should still get them to quote a price before driving off. You will be charged around 15 euros for the journey between Firá and the airport, and around 20 euros from Firá to Athínios Port.

HIGHWAY CODE

The maximum speed in built-up areas is 50kph (30mph) and on national roads 90kph (55mph). It is compulsory to wear seatbelts in the front seats. The drink-driving limit is 0.5 g of blood alcohol per litre for car drivers and 0.2 g for moped riders. Helmets must be worn on motorbikes. Heavy fines are enforced for traffic offences: illegal parking will cost you at least 60 euros.

FESTIVALS & EVENTS
ALL YEAR ROUND

Ágios Christodoulos

FEBRUARY/MARCH

Shrove Monday (all coastal villages): Outdoor picnics and kite-flying are organised on the beaches.

APRIL/MAY

Good Friday The *Epitafios,* an imitation of Christ's funeral bier, is decorated with flowers by local women in all parishes and paraded through the island's villages at night.

Easter Saturday Mass at 11pm. Shortly before midnight, all the lights in the churches are put out except for the Holy flame. The priest announces the resurrection of Christ at midnight and all worshippers light their candles.

Easter Sunday (Karterádos and all island villages): Spit-roast lamb and kid goat, followed by music, dancing and singing.

21 May Parish festival held in the morning at the Panagía Episkopí Church near Mésa Goniá.

JUNE

Supa Dupa Fly London's biggest hip-hop and R'n'B party takes place in many locations on Santorini. With live acts, beach parties, karaoke and yoga. *supadupaflysantorini.com*

AUGUST

Kímisis tis Theotókou The biggest religious festival of the summer takes places on 15th August, with live music, dancing and food, in Akrotíri and Mégalochóri.

SEPTEMBER

International Music Festival
International musicians (jazz and classical) gather for six concerts at the Nómikos Conference Centre between Firá and Imerovígli. *santorini.net.*

OCTOBER

Santorini Experience A three-day sporting event with swimming competitions in the caldera, plus fun runs. *santorini-experience.com*

EMERGENCIES

CONSULATES & EMBASSIES
British Embassy
1 Ploutarchou | 10675 Athens | tel. 21 07 27 26 00 | ukingreece.fco.gov.uk

Canadian Embassy
48 Eth. Antistaseos | 15231 Athens | tel. 21 07 27 34 00 | canadainternational. gc.ca/greece-grece

Irish Embassy
7 Leo. Vasileos Konstantinou | 10674 Athens | tel. 21 07 23 27 71 | dfa.ie/ irish-embassy/greece

US Embassy
91 Vasilissis Sofias | 11521 Athens | tel. 21 07 21 29 51 | AthensAmEmb@state. gov | athens.usembassy.gov

EMERGENCY SERVICES
Call 112 – for the police, fire brigade and ambulance.

HEALTH
Well-trained doctors guarantee basic medical care throughout Santorini, however there is often a lack of technical equipment. The state-run *Santorini Hospital (tel. 22 86 03 53 00 | santorini-hospital.gr)* in Karterádos has several specialist departments and is always open.

Emergency hospital treatment and by doctors is free of charge if you present the European Health Insurance Card (EHIC) or the Global Health Insurance Card (GHIC) issued by the UK government. However, in practice, doctors do so reluctantly and it is advisable to take out international health insurance; you can then choose your doctor, pay in cash, get a receipt and then present your bills to your insurance company for a refund.

Chemists are well stocked but they may not always have British medication. There are three chemists around the main square in Firá, and others in Emborió, Kamári and Messariá.

ESSENTIALS

ACCOMMODATION
There is a big selection of mostly small hotels which are quickly booked up in peak season. There are simple B&Bs in an inland village or near the beach, as well as luxury hotels in breathtakingly beautiful villages off the beaten track around the caldera and coastline.

A special treat is staying in a lava cave directly on the caldera's wall, although this will come at a price. In many cases, the centre of the village can only be reached from lava caves via stairs and steep paths, but most hotels offer a porter service.

There are two campsites: one at the bottom of Firá and the other on Períssa Beach. Santorini has no youth hostels and wild camping is prohibited.

To get an overview, it is best to visit large booking websites. Often, it is possible to book a room directly from the hotel or business-owner, although this is seldom the cheaper option.

BEACHES

Travellers looking for a beach holiday in the Aegean will find more suitable destinations than Santorini. The caldera side has no beaches and only a few points where you can access the water (at Oía and Akrotíri).

Some of the beaches on the Aegean side are very rocky or covered in coarse lava sand – flip flops or swim shoes are essential. Most beaches also have a steep slope into the water, making them unsuitable for young children and non-swimmers. Only the busy beaches have lifeguard posts (Kamári, Períssa, Perívolos, Monólithos), but they are not always manned.

Nude bathing is officially prohibited in Greece with the exception of a few beaches on Crete, Rhodes and Mykonos. This law is strictly applied on Santorini, but topless sunbathing is accepted.

CUSTOMS

EU citizens can import and export for their personal use tax-free: 800 cigarettes, 1kg tobacco, 90 litres of wine, 10 litres of spirits over 22%, 110 litres of beer. Non-EU citizens can import and export for their personal use tax-free: 200 cigarettes, 250g tobacco, 4 litres of wine, 1 litre of spirits over 22%, 16 litres of beer. *https://greece.visahq.com/customs*

DRINKING WATER

Outside Firá and Oía the tap water is not suitable for drinking, but can be used for cleaning teeth and washing fruit. Most of the water in Oía and Firá comes from the desalination plants, while elsewhere it comes from groundwater wells. Tasty it is not – wherever you are on the island.

ENTRY FEES & PRICES

Basic hotel rooms and apartments, as well as public transport, are considerably cheaper than in the UK, yet restaurants, petrol and food tend to be more expensive than at home.

HOW MUCH DOES IT COST?	
Coffee	4 euros *for a cappuccino*
Wine	from 5 euros *for a glass of house wine*
Wellness	20 euros *for a 30-min foot spa*
Snack	2.50 euros *for a gyros*
Petrol	1.70 euros *for 1 litre super unleaded*
Excursion	49 euros *for an island tour by bus and boat*

Entry to the excavations of Akrotíri and Ancient Thera and the Prehistoric Museum in Firá is free for concessions when a "special ticket package" is purchased for all three sites. Admission is free to everyone on the first Sunday of the month (November to March), on public holidays, on 6 March, on the last weekend in September, on International Monuments Day (April) and on International Museums Day (May).

INFORMATION

There is no official tourist information centre on the island. In high summer, an information kiosk in the *platía* of Firá is staffed on and off, but has very little information to give out. The official website of the island community, *santorini.gr*, is only up to date in parts; information given by this site should be checked carefully for accuracy. The website of the Greek Tourist Board is *visitgreece.com*.

GREEK ALPHABET

A	α	a	N	ν	n
B	β	v, w	Ξ	ξ	ks, x
Γ	γ	g, i	O	o	o
Δ	δ	d	Π	π	p
E	ε	e	P	ρ	r
Z	ζ	s, z	Σ	σ, ς	s, ss
H	η	i	T	τ	t
Θ	θ	th	Y	υ	i, y
I	ι	i, j	Φ	φ	f
K	κ	k	X	χ	ch
Λ	λ	l	Ψ	ψ	ps
M	μ	m	Ω	ώ	o

WEATHER

High season
Low season

	JAN	FEB	MAR	APRIL	MAY	JUNE	JULY	AUG	SEPT	OCT	NOV	DEC
Daytime temperates (°C)	15°	15°	17°	20°	24°	28°	31°	31°	28°	24°	20°	17°
Night-time temperatures (°C)	9°	9°	10°	13°	16°	20°	22°	23°	21°	17°	13°	10°
Hours of sunshine per day	5	5	7	9	10	12	13	12	11	8	6	4
Rainfall days per month	12	9	7	3	2	0	0	0	1	5	6	11
Sea temperature in °C	17	16	16	17	19	21	23	25	24	22	20	18

Hours of sunshine per day   Rainfall days per month   Sea temperature in °C

LANGUAGE

The Greeks are proud of their unique alphabet. Although place names and labels are often also written in Roman letters, it is still useful to have some knowledge of the Greek alphabet – and you really need to know how to stress the words correctly to be understood. The vowel with the accent is emphasised. However, there is no uniform transliteration, so expect to encounter a place name in three or four different versions.

LEFT LUGGAGE

You can leave your luggage at the bus terminal kiosk for 1 euro per hour.

MONEY

There are more cash machines than churches on Santorini; you can withdraw money with your credit or debit card. You will be charged 4–6 euros every time you take money from cash machines, regardless of the amount.

NATIONAL HOLIDAYS

1 Jan	New Year's Day
6 Jan	Epiphany
25 March	Independence Day; Annunciation Day
March / April	Good Friday; Easter
1 May	Labour Day
June	Whitsun
15 Aug	Assumption Day
28 Oct	National Holiday
25 / 26 Dec	Christmas

POST

There are post offices and agencies in Firá, Akrotíri, Kamári, Messariá, Oía and Teríssa. They are open Mon–Fri, 7.30am–3pm.

TELEPHONE & WIFI

Mobile coverage on the entire island is excellent. You should be able to make calls, text and surf the web in Greece, subject to the conditions of your local mobile phone operator. The country code for Greece is 0030 followed by the full telephone number. When making a call from Santorini, dial 0044 for the UK; 00353 for Ireland; 001 for the US and Canada; 0061 for Australia; then dial the local code without "0" and then the individual number.

Fast and free-of-charge WiFi is available in most of the island's cafés, bars and restaurants. A lot of hotels offer guests free WiFi but some of the more expensive hotels charge for this.

TIPPING

In restaurants you do not round up the bill when paying but wait until your change is returned and give a tip or leave it on the table when you leave. Taxi drivers and chamber maids are also pleased to receive tips, but please note that anything less than 1 euro is seen as rather offensive.

TOILETS

Please never put loo paper down the loo, but always into a dustbin or bucket next to it. This also applies in luxury hotels and restaurants. Many toilets are modern and very clean, but public conveniences are rare. The only one that is well maintained is at the Firá bus terminal.

HOLIDAY VIBES

FOR RELAXATION AND CHILLING

FOR BOOKWORMS AND FILM BUFFS

📖 THE SANTORINI ODYSSEY

A novel by Peg Maddocks in which four Americans participate in the exploration of a cave in the ruins of Ancient Thera on Santorini. It also retells the story of a number of Greek myths (2004).

📖 A MARKER TO MEASURE DRIFT

A hypnotic novel by Alexander Maksik about a young Liberian woman living in a beach cave on Santorini who slowly has to come to terms with her past (2013).

🎥 MAMMA MIA!

The Abba musical with Meryl Streep and Pierce Brosnan was actually filmed on Skópelos and Skiáthos in 2008, but it gives you a very good idea of the general Greek way of life. Cíne Kamári on Santorini shows this film on a regular basis.

🎥 SMALL CRIME

A very funny film by Cypriot director Chrístos Georgíou which was filmed in 2008 on Santorini's sister island of Thirasía. You get a good impression of the landscape around the caldera, as well as the lively and joyous temperament of the Greeks.

0:58

II MÍKIS THEODORÁKIS – ZORBA'S DANCE
The most famous of all *syrtákis*. Played almost continuously in many tavernas.

▶ VANGÉLIS – HYMNE
The perfect electronic soundtrack for the sunset on Santorini.

▶ SYLLOGIKÓ ERGÓ – DÍRLADA
A popular tune of the sponge fishermen from the island of Kálymnos – great for dancing along to!

▶ MANÓLIS KALOMÍRIS – TRIPTYCH
This is a bit different: a symphony by one of the most important classical composers of Greece.

Your holiday soundtrack can be found on **Spotify** *under* **MARCO POLO** *Greece*

Or scan this code with the Spotify app

ONLINE

AEGEAN DIVERS
This app was designed by the Aegean Divers centre to provide interesting and important information on the island's diving spots, sea life and underwater photos and videos.

GTP.GR
Ideal for looking up ferry connections.

ODYSSEUS.CULTURE.GR
This official homepage of the Greek Ministry of Culture publishes information about opening times and admission fees for all archaeological sites and state-run museums across the country, including on Santorini.

MARINE TRAFFIC
This app is essential if you want to know where the many cruise ships and ferries in the caldera have come from or are sailing to.

SANTORINI GREECE
This app (available at a cost) includes extensive information on all resorts, sights and beaches as well as price comparisons for hotels.

USEFUL WORDS & PHRASES

SMALLTALK

Yes/no/maybe	ne/ˈochi/ˈissos	Ναι/ Όχι/Ισως
Please/Thank you	parakaˈlo/efcharisˈto	Παρακαλώ/ Ευχαριστώ
Good morning/good evening/goodnight!	kalliˈmera/kalliˈspera/ kalliˈnichta!	Καλήέραμ/ Καλησπέρα!/ Καληνύχτα!
Hello/ goodbye (formal)/ goodbye (informal)!	ˈya (su/sass)/ aˈdio/ ya (su/sass)!	Γεία (σου/σας)!/ αντίο!/Γεία (σου/ σας)!
My name is …	me ˈlene …	Με λένεÖ …
What's your name?	poss sass ˈlene?	Πως σας λένε;
Excuse me/sorry	me sigˈchorite/ sigˈnomi	Με συγχωρείτε / Συγνώμ
Pardon?	oˈriste?	Ορίστε;
I (don't) like this	Afˈto (dhen) mu aˈressi	Αυτό (δεν) ουμ αρέσει

SYMBOLS

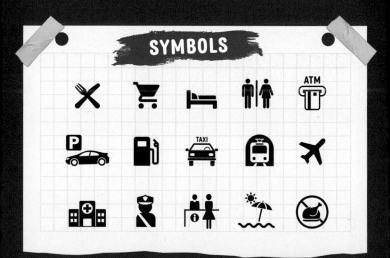

EATING & DRINKING

Could you please book a table for tonight for four?	Klis'te mass parakal'lo 'enna tra'pezi ya a'popse ya 'tessera 'atoma	Κλείστε αςμ παρακαλώ ένα τραπέζι γιά απόψε γιά τέσσερα άτοαμ
The menu, please	tonn ka'taloggo parakal'lo	Τον κατάλογο παρακαλώ
Could I please have … ?	tha 'ithella na 'echo …?	Θα ήθελα να έχο …?
More/less	pjo/li'gotäre	ρπιό/λιγότερο
with/without ice/ sparkling	me/cho'ris 'pa-go/ anthrakik'ko	εμ/χωρίς πάγο/ ανθρακικό
(un)safe drinking water	(mi) 'possimo nä'ro	(μη) Πόσιμο νερό
vegetarian/allergy	chorto'fagos/allerg'ia	Χορτοφάγος/ Αλλεργία
May I have the bill, please?	'thel'lo na pli'rosso parakal'lo	Θέλω να πληρώσω παρακαλώ

MISCELLANEOUS

Where is …?	pu tha vro …?	Που θα βρω …?
What time is it?	Ti 'ora 'ine?	Τι ώρα είναι?
How much does… cost ?	Posso 'kani …?	Πόσο κάνει …?
Where can I find internet access?	pu bor'ro na vro 'prosvassi sto índernett?	Που πορώμ να βρω πρόσβαση στο ίντερνετ?
pharmacy/ chemist	farma'kio/ ka'tastima	Φαρακείομ/ Κατάστημ καλλυντικών
fever/pain /diarrhoea/ nausea	piret'tos/'ponnos/ dhi'arria/ana'gula	Πυρετός/Πόνος/ Διάρροια/Αναγούλα
Help!/Watch out! Be Careful	Wo'ithia!/Prosso'chi!/ Prosso'chi!	Βοήθεια!/Προσοχή!/ Προσοχή!
Forbidden/banned	apa'goräfsi/ apago'räwäte	Απαγόρευση/ απαγορέυεται
0/1/2/3/4/5/6/7/8/9/ 10/100/1000	mi'dhen / 'enna / 'dhio / 'tria / 'tessera / 'pende /'eksi / ef'ta / och'to / e'nea / dhekka / eka'to / 'chilia / 'dhekka chil'iades	ηδένμ/ένα/δύο/τρία/ τέσσερα/πέντε/έξι/ εφτά/οχτώ/ εννέα/ δέκα/εκατό/χίλια/ δέκα χιλιάδες

TRAVEL PURSUIT

THE MARCO POLO HOLIDAY QUIZ

Do you know your facts about Santorini? Here you can test your knowledge of the little secrets and idiosyncrasies of the island and its people. You will find the correct answers below, with further details on pages 18 to 23 of this guide.

❶ What are the Greek-Orthodox priests officially called who are easily identified by their magnificent beards, long hair and stiff hat?
a) Pope
b) Pappás
c) Prometheus

❷ What is the Greek word for a female Saint? You also find this word in the names of many churches and convents.
a) Ágii
b) Agía
c) Panagía

❸ How many annual overnight stays in hotels, B&Bs, apartments and camp sites does Santorini record?
a) approx. 60,000
b) approx. 600,000
c) approx. 6 million

❹ Soil taken from Santorini was used to build which canal in the 19th century?
a) Suez Canal in Egypt
b) Grand Union Canal in the UK
c) Corinth Canal in Greece

Answers: 1b, 2b, 3c, 4a, 5c, 6c, 7a, 8b, 9c, 10b

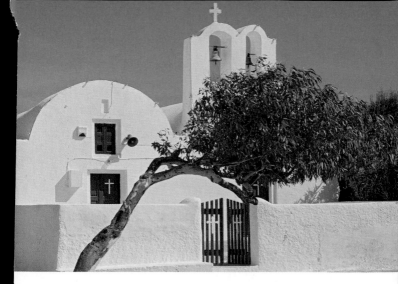

The church of Ágios Geórgios in Oía is one of many dedicated to the saint

❺ What do Greeks call the north wind which is often strong but also refreshingly cool in summer?
a) Sirocco
b) Typhoon
c) Meltémi

❻ What does the island's power station at Monólithos use to produce 120,000 megawatts of electricity each year?
a) Uranium fission
b) Olive oil
c) Masut

❼ When was the Greek state within its current borders founded?
a) In 1947
b) In 1821
c) At the time of Christ's birth

❽ You'll often hear the Greek word "Entáxi" – what does it mean?
a) A taxi
b) Okay
c) Absolutely not

❾ Which colours are many of the island's tavernas painted in?
a) An earthy brown and muddy grey
b) Orange and yellow
c) White and blue

❿ When did the Ottomans destroy the Byzantine Empire by capturing Constantinople (today's Istanbul)?
a) In 1054
b) In 1453
c) In 1912

INDEX

INDEX & CREDITS

WE WANT TO HEAR FROM YOU!

Did you have a great holiday? Is there something on your mind? Whatever it is, let us know! Whether you want to praise the guide, alert us to errors or give us a personal tip – MARCO POLO would be pleased to hear from you.

We do everything we can to provide the very latest information for your trip. Nevertheless, despite all of our authors' thorough research, errors can creep in. MARCO POLO does not accept any liability for this. Please contact us by e-mail.

e-mail: sales@heartwoodpublishing.co.uk

Picture credits

Cover: Oía church's belltower (istock/guenterguni) Photographs: K. Bötig (135); huber-images: G. Filippini (42, 92), G. Gräfenhain (6/7, 108/109), M. Liebrecht (26/27), M. Rellini (130/131), M. Ripani (11, 74); Laif: C. Heeb (12/13, 103), M. Jäger (19, 107); Laif/ Le Figaro Magazine: Fabre (24/25, 70); Laif/Loop Images: E. Nathan (120/121); Laif/Polaris: M. Kouri (94); Laif/robertharding: N. Clark (96/97), S. Papadopoulos (90), M. Parry (2/3); Look: H. Bias (20), H. Leue (104); mauritius images: G. Gräfenhain (54), R. Hackenberg (123); mauritius images/AGF: V. Valletta (outer front flap, inner front flap/1); mauritius images/ Alamy: AegeanPhoto (101), H. Corneli (80/81), M. Fairman (8), M. Gonda (48), Hackenberg-Photo-Cologne (57), B. Kean (119), W. Linden (58/59, 79), A. McAulay (45), J. Sedmak (132/133); mauritius images/ Cultura: G. u. M. David de Lossy (32/33); mauritius images/hemis.fr (27); mauritius images/Image Source (10); mauritius images/imagebroker: C. Handl (23); mauritius images/Pitopia (9); picture-alliance: R. Hackenberg (31, 53, 65); picture-alliance/APA/picture-desk.com: F. Pritz (30/31, 35); picture-alliance/Arco Images (51); picture-alliance/imagebroker: C. Handl (73); picture-alliance/SZ Photo: M. Neubauer (77); pic-ture-alliance/ZB: D. Gammert (46/47); Schapowalow: G. Cozzi (14/15, 38/39); Shutterstock: FotoHelin (66), proslgn (89), A. Todorovic (87), G. Tsichlis (68), I. Woolcock (Klappe hinten); vario images/imagebroker (113). Shutterstock.com: Ludovic Farine (28), Vladimir1984 (35)

2nd Edition – fully revised and updated 2022
Worldwide Distribution: Heartwood Publishing Ltd, Bath, United Kingdom
www.heartwoodpublishing.co.uk

© MAIRDUMONT GmbH & Co. KG, Ostfildern
Author: Klaus Bötig; **Editors**: Franziska Kahl, Arnd M. Schuppius
Picture editor: Anja Schlatterer
Cartography: © MAIRDUMONT, Ostfildern (pp. 36-37, 110, back cover, pull-out map);
© MAIRDUMONT, Ostfildern, using map data from OpenStreetMap, Lizenz CC-BY-SA 2.0 (pp. 40–41, 60–61, 63, 69, 82–83, 84, 95, 98–99).
Cover design and pull out map cover design: bilekjaeger_Kreativagentur mit Zukunftswerkstatt, with Zukunftswerkstatt, Stuttgart; **page designs**: Langenstein Communication GmbH, Ludwigsburg
Text on the back flap: Lucia Rojas

Heartwood Publishing credits:
Translated from the German by Thomas Moser and Susan Jones
Editors: Kate Michell and Sophie Blacksell Jones
Prepress: Summerlane Books, Bath
Printed in India

All rights reserved. No part of this book may be repro-duced, stored in a retrieval system or transmitted in any form or by any means (electronic, mechanical, photocopying, recording or otherwise) without prior written permission from the publisher

MARCO POLO AUTHOR
KLAUS BÖTIG

This travel journalist is convinced that you have to visit Santorini at least once in your life. Despite the tourist hordes, he knows where to find quiet villages, wild landscapes and remote beaches where you can enjoy the beauty of this special island undisturbed. He also knows the really good tavernas where the locals like to eat.

135

DOS & DON'TS!

HOW TO AVOID SLIP-UPS AND BLUNDERS

DO SHOW MODERATION WHEN WINE TASTING

Do not go overboard when wine tasting: if you keep topping up your glass and then drive a car or moped, you will easily exceed the drink-driving limit (0.5g or 0.2g of blood alcohol per litre respectively). Greece has high fines for traffic offences and you may also have your licence revoked.

DON'T SPEND TOO MUCH

Don't be sold an organised excursion on your very first day. You will soon notice that you can get to most places on the island by public bus, and that taxi rides are often cheaper if there are four of you travelling.

DON'T EXPECT FRESH CALAMARI

Many tourists and Greeks love eating calamari. It is very tasty, but seldom comes from the Mediterranean or the Aegean. It is usually imported from the Far East. Try some of the locally caught fish instead.

DON'T BUY LAVA JEWELLERY

The lava jewellery on sale all over the island has little to do with Santorini. It is made from ground lava which is then shaped and imported from the other side of the world. A Swiss company specialises in the production.

DON'T BE SHOCKED BY THE PRICE OF FISH

Fresh fish is very expensive and is sold by weight. Always ask for the kilo price first and when the fish is being weighed, make sure you are present to avoid any unpleasant surprises on the bill.